ACCUPLACER®
Math Workbook

Everything You Need to Practice, Learn, and Ace the Exam

Copyright © 2026 by Complete Test Preparation Inc. ALL RIGHTS RESERVED.

Intellectual Property Rights This publication is protected by copyright. No part of this book may be reproduced, copied, distributed, or transmitted in any form or by any means—including graphic, electronic, or mechanical methods such as photocopying, recording, or information storage and retrieval systems—without the prior written permission of the publisher, except in the case of brief quotations embodied in critical reviews and certain other noncommercial uses permitted by copyright law.

Disclaimer & Limitation of Liability While the publisher and author have used their best efforts in preparing this book, they make no representations or warranties with respect to the accuracy or completeness of the contents. The advice and strategies contained herein may not be suitable for your situation. Test content and administration rules change frequently; readers are advised to verify all information with the official test providers. Complete Test Preparation Inc. shall not be liable for any loss of profit or any other commercial damages, including but not limited to special, incidental, consequential, or other damages.

Non-Affiliation Notice Complete Test Preparation Inc. is an independent publisher and is not affiliated with, endorsed by, or sponsored by any testing organization, educational institution, or government agency mentioned in this publication. All trademarks, service marks, and trade names are the property of their respective owners and are used for reference and identification purposes only..

We strongly recommend that students check with exam providers for up-to-date information regarding test content.

ACCUPLACER® is a registered trademark of ACT Inc., who are not involved in the production of, and do not endorse this publication.

Published by
Complete Test Preparation Inc.

Visit us on the web at
https://www.test-preparation.ca

ISBN-13: 9781772451641
Version April 5, 2026

About Complete Test Preparation Inc.

Why Choose Complete Test Preparation? You want to spend your valuable study time where it counts the most. We've got you covered.

Since 2005, we have helped hundreds of thousands of students succeed with over 145 study guides and online courses. We know that tests change, which is why we keep our content current and relevant.

Study with a Purpose With this purchase, you are doing more than just preparing for a test. You are supporting a mission to improve education globally. We are proud to support charities that bring learning opportunities to those who need them most.

Learn more about our mission:
https://www.test-preparation.ca/charities-and-non-profits/

You have definitely come to the right place.
If you want to spend your valuable study time where it will help you the most - we've got you covered today and tomorrow.

Thank you for studying with us!

Feedback

Continuous Improvement. We strive to keep our materials as up-to-date as possible. If you spot an error or have a suggestion, let us know at feedback@test-preparation.ca. We take feedback seriously. Unlike traditional publishers, our Print-on-Demand model allows us to implement updates and improvements frequently.

https://www.youtube.com/user/MrTestPreparation

Contents

9   **The Game Plan: Your Accuplacer Roadmap**
      The ACCUPLACER® Study Plan   11
      Making a Study Schedule   12

18   **The Foundations: Mastering the Essentials**
      Fraction Tips, Tricks and Short-cuts   19
      Decimal Tips, Tricks and Short-cuts   24
      Converting Decimals to Fractions   25
      Percent Tips, Tricks and Short-cuts   27
      Scientific Notation   30
      How to Convert to Scientific Notation   31
      Exponents and Radicals   33
      Exponents: Tips, Short-cuts & Tricks   33
      Simplifying Radicals   36
      Basic Math Practice   38
      Answer Key   50

57   **Translating the Text: Cracking Word Problems**
      How to Solve Word Problems   58
      Types of Word Problems   61
      Word Problem Practice with Video   72
      Most Common Word Problem Mistakes   73
      Word Problem Practice   75
      Answer Key   83

95   **Shapes and Space: Navigating Geometry**
      Pythagorean Geometry   101
      Quadrilaterals   104
      Geometry Practice Questions   113
      Answer Key   136

150   **The Power of X: Building Your Algebra Core**
      Solving One-Variable Linear Equations   151
      Solving Two-Variable Linear Equations   152
      Simplifying Polynomials   153
      Factoring Polynomials   154

	Quadratic Equations	155
	Quadratic Word Problems	157
	Common Algebra Mistakes on Tests	159
	Basic Algebra Practice	163
	Answer Key	176

202	**Next Level Logic: Advanced Algebra & Functions**	
	Trigonometry - A Quick Tutorial	203
	Logarithms - A Quick Tutorial	204
	Sequences - A Quick Tutorial	206
	Advanced Algebra Practice	209
	Answer Key	219

| 236 | **The Kitchen Table Guide: How to Actually Study Math** | |

240	**Smart Strategy: Pre-Game Prep for Success**	
	Phase 1: The Setup	241
	Phase 2: The Study Strategy	242
	Phase 3: Mental & Physical Readiness	244
	The Anti-Procrastination Rule	244
	Psych Yourself Up (Not Out)	244

246	**Test-Day Tactics: Staying Sharp Under Pressure**	
	Master the Exam	246
	Phase 1: The Arrival and Setup	247
	Phase 2: The Launch	248
	Phase 3: Answering Strategies	249
	Phase 4: The Review	251
	Common Accuplacer Pitfalls (And How to Dodge Them)	253

| 256 | **You've Done the Work—Now Go Own the Result** |
| 257 | **The Toolbox: Digital Extras & Practice Portals** |

The Game Plan: Your Accuplacer Roadmap

Getting Started

CONGRATULATIONS! By deciding to take the ACCU-PLACER® you have taken the first step toward a great future! Of course, there is no point in taking this important examination unless you intend to do your best to earn the highest grade that you possibly can. That means getting yourself organized and discovering the best approaches, methods and strategies to master the material. Yes, that will require real effort and dedication on your part, but if you are willing to focus your energy and devote the study time necessary, before you know it you will be passing the ACCUPLACER® with a great score!

ACCUPLACER® Math Practice

We know that taking on a new endeavor can be scary, and it is easy to feel unsure of where to begin. That's where we come in. This workbook is designed to help you improve your test-taking skills, show you a few tricks of the trade and increase both your competency and confidence.

The ACCUPLACER® Exam Math Content

Numerical Skills

- Scientific Notation
- Exponents and Radicals
- Square Root
- Fractions, Decimals and Percent
- Means, Median and Modes

Algebra

- Solve real world problems with ratio and proportion
- Solve one and two variable equations
- Identify and solve quadratic equations given values or graphs
- Solve quadratic using different methods
- Translate real world problems into quadratic equations and solve

Advanced Algebra

- Trigonometry
- Logarithms
- Sequences

Simple Geometry

Slope of a line
Identify linear equations from a graph
Calculate perimeter, circumference and volume
Solve problems using the Pythagorean theorem
Determine geometric transformations
Solve real world problems using the properties of geometric shapes

The ACCUPLACER® Study Plan

Now that you have made the decision to take the ACCUPLACER®, it is time to get started. Before you do another thing, you will need to figure out a plan of attack. The best study tip is to start early! The longer the time period you devote to regular study practice, the more likely you will be to retain the material and be able to access it quickly. If you thought that 1 x 20 is the same as 2 x 10, guess what? It really is not, when it comes to study time. Reviewing material for just an hour per day over the course of 20 days is far better than studying for two hours a day for only 10 days. The more often you revisit a particular piece of information, the better you will know it. Not only will your grasp and understanding improve, but your ability to reach into your brain and quickly and efficiently pull out the tidbit you need, will be greatly enhanced as well.

The great Chinese scholar and philosopher Confucius believed that true knowledge could be defined as knowing both what you know and what you do not know. The first step in preparing for the ACCUPLACER® is to assess your strengths and weaknesses. You may already have an idea of what you know and what you do not know, but evaluating yourself for each of the math areas will clarify the details.

ACCUPLACER® Math Practice

Making a Study Schedule

To make your study time the most productive, you will need to develop a study plan. The purpose of the plan is to organize all the bits of pieces of information in such a way that you will not feel overwhelmed. Rome was not built in a day, and learning everything you will need to know to pass the ACCUPLACER® is going to take time, too. Arranging the material you need to learn into manageable chunks is the best way to go. Each study session should make you feel as though you have accomplished your goal, and your goal is simply to learn what you planned to learn during that particular session. Try to organize the content in such a way that each study session builds on previous ones. That way, you will retain the information, be better able to access it, and review the previous bits and pieces at the same time.

Self-assessment

The Best Study Tip! The best study tip is to start early! The longer you study regularly, the more you will retain and 'learn' the material. Studying for 1 hour per day for 20 days is far better than studying for 2 hours for 10 days.

What don't you know?

The first step is to assess your strengths and weaknesses. You may already have an idea of where your weaknesses are, or you can take our Self-assessment modules for each of the areas, Reading Comprehension, Arithmetic, Essay Writing, Algebra and College Level Math.

Exam Component	Rate 1 to 5
Arithmetic	
Decimals Percent and Fractions	
Problem solving (Word Problems)	
Basic Algebra	
Simple Geometry	
Problem Solving	
Algebra	
Exponents	
Linear Equations	
Quadratics	
Polynomials	
College Level	
Coordinate Geometry	
Trigonometry	
Logarithms	
Sequences	

Making a Study Schedule

The key to a study plan is to divide the material you need to learn into manageable size and learn it, while at the same time reviewing the material that you already know.

Using the table above, any scores of three or below, you need to spend time learning, going over, and practicing this subject area. A score of four means you need to review the material, but you don't have to spend time re-learning. A score of five and you are OK with just an occasional review before the exam.

A score of zero or one means you really do need to work on this and you should allocate the most time and give it the highest priority. Some students prefer a 5-day plan and others a 10-day plan. It also depends on how much time until the exam.

Here is an example of a 5-day plan based on an example from the table above:

Trigonometry: 1   Study 1 hour everyday – review on last day
Fractions: 3   Study 1 hour for 2 days then ½ hour and then review
Algebra: 4   Review every second day
Polynomials: 2 Study 1 hour on the first day – then ½ hour everyday
Sequences: 5   Review for ½ hour every other day
Geometry: 5 Review for ½ hour every other day

Using this example, geometry and sequences are good and only need occasional review. Algebra is good and needs 'some' review. Fractions need a bit of work, polynomials needs a lot of work and trigonometry is very weak and need most of time. Based on this, here is a sample study plan:

Getting Started

Day	Subject	Time
Monday		
Study	Trigonometry	1 hour
Study	Polynomials	1 hour
	½ hour break	
Study	Fractions	1 hour
Review	Algebra	½ hour
Tuesday		
Study	Trigonometry	1 hour
Study	Polynomials	½ hour
	½ hour break	
Study	Fractions	½ hour
Review	Algebra	½ hour
Review	Geometry	½ hour
Wednesday		
Study	Trigonometry	1 hour
Study	Polynomials	½ hour
	½ hour break	
Study	Fractions	½ hour
Review	Geometry	½ hour
Thursday		
Study	Trigonometry	½ hour
Study	Polynomials	½ hour
Review	Fractions	½ hour
	½ hour break	
Review	Geometry	½ hour
Review	Algebra	½ hour
Friday		
Review	Trigonometry	½ hour
Review	Polynomials	½ hour
Review	Fractions	½ hour
	½ hour break	
Review	Algebra	½ hour
Review	Polynomials	½ hour

Using this example, adapt the study plan to your own schedule. This schedule assumes 2 ½ - 3 hours available to study everyday for a 5 day period.

First, write out what you need to study and how much. Next figure out how many days before the test. Note, do NOT study on the last day before the test. On the last day before the test, you won't learn anything and will probably only confuse yourself.

Make a table with the days before the test and the number of hours you have available to study each day. We suggest working with 1 hour and ½ hour time slots.

Start filling in the blanks, with the subjects you need to study the most getting the most time and the most regular time slots (i.e. everyday) and the subjects that you know getting the least time (e.g. ½ hour every other day, or every 3rd day).

Tips for making a schedule

Once you make a schedule, stick with it! Make your study sessions reasonable. If you make a study schedule and don't stick with it, you set yourself up for failure. Instead, schedule study sessions that are a bit shorter and set yourself up for success! Make sure your study sessions are do-able. Studying is hard work, but after you pass, you can party and take a break!

Schedule breaks. Breaks are just as important as study time. Work out a rotation of studying and breaks that works for you.

Build up study time. If you find it hard to sit still and study for 1 hour straight through, build up to it. Start with 20 minutes, and then take a break. Once you get used to 20-minute study sessions, increase the time to 30 minutes. Gradually work you way up to 1 hour.

40 minutes to 1 hour is optimal. Studying for longer than this is tiring and not productive. Studying for shorter isn't long enough to be productive.

How to Study
For more information, see our How to Study Guide at
https://www.test-preparation.ca/learning-study/

Flash Cards - The Complete Guide

https://www.test-preparation.ca/flash-cards/

The Foundations: Mastering the Essentials

Basic Math

Basic Math

The Basic Math section covers:

- Fractions, Decimals and Percent
- Scientific Notation
- Exponents and Radicals

Fraction Tips, Tricks and Short-cuts

When you are writing an exam, time is precious, so anything you can do to answer questions faster is a real advantage.

Here are some ideas, Short-cuts, tips and tricks that can speed up answering fraction problems.

Remember that a fraction is just a number which names a portion of something. For instance, instead of having a whole pie, a fraction says you have a part of a pie--such as a half of one or a fourth of one.

Two numbers make up a fraction. The number on top is the numerator. The number on the bottom is the denominator.

To remember which is which, just remember that "denominator" and "down" both start with a "d." And the "downstairs" number is the denominator. So for instance, in ½, the numerator is 1, and the denominator (or "downstairs") number is 2.

Adding Fractions

It's easy to add two fractions if they have the same denominator. Just add the digits on top and leave the bottom one the same: 1/10 + 6/10 = 7/10.

It's the same with subtracting fractions with the same denominator: 7/10 - 6/10 = 1/10.

Adding and subtracting fractions with different denominators is a little more complicated.

First, you have to arrange the fractions so they have the same denominators.

The easiest way to do this is to multiply the

denominators: For 2/5 + 1/2 multiply 5 by 2. Now you have a denominator of 10.

But now you have to change the top numbers too. Since you multiplied the 5 in 2/5 by 2, you also multiply the 2 by 2, to get 4. So the first fraction is now 4/10.

In the second fraction, you multiplied the denominator by 5, you have to multiply the numerator by 5 also, to get 5/10.

Now you have 4/10 + 5/10 and you can add 5 and 4 to get 9/10.

Simplest Form

To reduce a fraction to its simplest form, you have to arrange the numerator and denominator so the only common factor is 1.

Think of it this way:

Let's take an example: The fraction 2/10.

This is not reduced to its simplest terms because there is a number that will divide evenly into both: 2. We want to make it so that the only number that will divide evenly into both is 1.

Divide the top and bottom by 2 to get the new, reduced fraction - 1/5.

Multiplying Fractions

This is the easiest of all: Just multiply the two top numbers and then multiply the two bottom numbers.

Here is an example,

2/5 X 2/3

First, multiply the numerators: 2 X 2 = 4

then multiply the denominators: 5 X 3 = 15

Your answer is 4/15.

Dividing Fractions

Dividing fractions is easy if you remember a simple trick - first turn the second fraction upside down - then multiply!

Here is an example:

7/8 X 1/2

Turn the second fraction upside down:

7/8 X 2/1

then multiply:
(7 X 2) / (8 X 1) = 14/8

Converting Fractions to Decimals

There are a couple of ways to convert fractions to decimals. The first, which is the fastest -- is to memorize some basic fraction facts.

1/100 is "one hundredth," expressed as a decimal, it's .01.

1/50 is "two hundredths," expressed as a decimal, it's .02.

1/25 is "one twenty-fifth" or "four hundredths," expressed as a decimal, it's .04.

1/20 is "one twentieth" or ""five hundredths," expressed as a decimal, it's .05.

1/10 is "one tenth," expressed as a decimal, it's .1.

1/8 is "one eighth," or "one hundred twenty-five

thousandths," expressed as a decimal, it's .125.

1/5 is "one fifth," or "two tenths," expressed as a decimal, it's .2.

1/4 is "one fourth" or "twenty-five hundredths," expressed as a decimal, it's .25.

1/3 is "one third" or "thirty-three hundredths," expressed as a decimal, it's .33.

1/2 is "one half" or "five tenths," expressed as a decimal, it's .5.

3/4 is "three fourths," or "seventy-five hundredths," expressed as a decimal, it's .75.

Of course, if you're no good at memorization, another good technique for converting a fraction to a decimal is to manipulate it so that the fraction's denominator is 10, 100, 1000, or some other power of 10.

Here's an example: We'll start with three quarters. What is the first number in the 4 "times table" that you can multiply and get a multiple of 10? Can you multiply 4 by something to get 10? No. Can you multiply it by something to get 100? Yes! 4 X 25 is 100.

So multiply the numerator by 25, which is 75 over 100

We know fractions are really a division problem, and we also know that dividing by 100, means we move the decimal 2 places to the left.

So, 75 over 100 = .75

Lets try another example - Convert one fifth to a decimal.

First find a power of 10 that 5 goes into evenly, which is 2.

Multiply the numerator and denominator by 2, which is two tenths.

Dividing 2 by 10 means we move the decimal place 1 place to the left.

So 1/5 = 0.5

Converting Fractions to Percent

Here is a quick method to convert fraction to percent and a strategy for answering on a multiple choice test that will save you valuable exam time.

First, remember that a fraction is a division problem: you're dividing the bottom number into the top.

Taking an example, convert 2/3 into percent.

The first method is to multiple the numerator by 100 and divide. So,

(2 X 100) / 2 = 100/3 = 66.66

Add a % sign and you have the answer, 66.66%

https://youtu.be/T9qiEHzwJEU?si=ZF9qVNLEF6JnPgqm

If you're doing these conversions on a multiple-choice test, here's an idea that might be even easier and faster. Let's say you have a fraction of 1/8 and you're asked to convert to percent.

Since we know that "percent" means hundredths, ask yourself what number we can multiply 8 by to get 100. Since there is no number, ask what number gets us close to 100.

── Basic Math ──

That number is 12: 8 X 12 = 96. So it gets us a little less than 100. Now, whatever you do to the denominator, you have to do to the numerator. Let's multiply 1 X 12 and we get 12. However, since 96 is a little less than 100, we know that our answer will be a little MORE than 12%.

Look at the choices and eliminate the obvious wrong choices. So if your possible answers on the multiple-choice test are these:

a) 8.5% b) 19% c)12.5% d) 25%

then we know the answer is c) 12.5%, because it's a little MORE than the 12 we got in our math problem above.

Here all the choices except choice C 12.5% can be eliminated.

You don't have to know the exact correct answer, just enough to estimate, then eliminate the obviously wrong answers.

This was an easy example to demonstrate the strategy, but don't be fooled! You probably won't get such an easy question on your exam. By estimating your answer quickly, then eliminating obviously incorrect choices immediately, you save precious exam time.

Decimal Tips, Tricks and Short-cuts

Converting Decimals to Fractions

Converting decimals to fractions is easy if you say it the

right way! If you say "point one" or "point 25," you'll have trouble.

But if you say, "one tenth" and "twenty-five hundredths," then you have already solved it! That's because, if you know your fractions, you know that "one tenth" looks like this: 1/10. And "twenty-five hundredths" looks like this: 25/100.

Even if you have digits before the decimal, such as 3.4, learning how to say the word will help you with the conversion into a fraction. It's not "three point four," it's "three and four tenths." Knowing this, you know that the fraction which looks like "three and four tenths" is 3 4/10.

The conversion is not complete until you reduce the fraction to its lowest terms: It's not 25/100, but 1/4.

Converting Decimals to Percent

Changing a decimal to a percent is easy if you remember one thing: multiply by 100.

For example, if you start with .45, simply multiply it by 100 for 45. Then add the % sign to the end - 45%.

Think of it this way: take out the decimal point, add a percent sign on the opposite side. In other words, the decimal on the left is replaced by the % on the right.

It doesn't work quite that easily if the decimal is in the middle of the number. For example, 3.7. Here, take out the decimal in the middle and replace it with a 0 % at the end. So 3.7 converted to decimal is 370%.

Percent Tips, Tricks and Short-cuts

Percent problems are not nearly as scary as they appear, if you remember this neat trick:

Draw a cross as in:

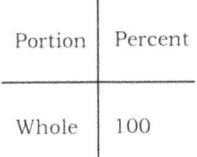

In the upper left, write PORTION. In the bottom left write WHOLE. In the top right, write PERCENT and in the bottom right, write 100. Whatever your problem is, you will leave blank the unknown, and fill in the other four parts. For example, let's suppose your problem is: Find 10% of 50. Since we know the 10% part, we put 10 in the percent corner. Since the whole number in our problem is 50, we put that in the corner marked whole. You always put 100 underneath the percent, so we leave it as is, which leaves only the top left corner blank. This is where we'll put our answer. Now simply multiply the two corner numbers that are NOT 100. Here, it's 10 X 50. That gives us 500. Now divide this by the remaining corner, or 100, to get a final answer of 5. 5 is the number that goes in the upper-left corner, and is your final solution.

Another hint to remember: Percents are the same thing as hundredths in decimals. So .45 is the same as 45 hundredths or 45 percent.

Percent Tips and Tricks Video

https://youtu.be/T9qiEHzwJEU?si=Vvo_WY8sdTPhF8S7

Converting Percents to Decimals

Percents are just a type of decimal, so it should be no surprise that converting between the two is actually fairly simple. Here are a few tricks and Short-cuts to keep in mind:

- Remember that percent literally means "per 100" or "for every 100." So when you speak of 30% you're saying 30 for every 100 or the fraction 30/100. In basic math, you learned that fractions

that have 10 or 100 as the denominator can easily be turned to a decimal. 30/100 is thirty hundredths, or expressed as a decimal, .30.
- Another way to look at it: To convert a percent to a decimal, simply divide the number by 100. So for instance, if the percent is 47%, divide 47 by 100. The result will be .47. Get rid of the % mark and you're done.
- Remember that the easiest way of dividing by 100 is by moving your decimal two spots to the left.

Converting Percents to Fractions

Converting percents to fractions is easy. After all, a percent is just a type of fraction; it tells you what part of 100 that you're talking about. Here are some simple ideas for making the conversion from a percent to a fraction:

- If the percent is a whole number -- say 34% -- then simply write a fraction with 100 as the denominator (the bottom number). Then put the percentage itself on top. So 34% becomes 34/100.
- Now reduce as you would reduce any percent. Here, by dividing 2 into 34 and 2 into 100, you get 17/50.
- If your percent is not a whole number -- say 3.4% --then convert it to a decimal expressed as hundredths. 3.4 is the same as 3.40 (or 3 and forty hundredths). Now ask yourself how you would express "three and forty hundredths" as a fraction. It would, of course, be 3 40/100. Reduce this and it becomes 3 2/5.

Scientific Notation

Science notation is a very simple and effective way of representing very large numbers in simpler forms. For example, instead of writing out 149,600,000,000 meters, which is the estimated distance from the sun, astronomers could easily write it out as 1.496×10^{11} meters.

Scientific notation expresses numbers in their powers of ten. It can also be used to express simple numbers. For example, using scientific notation, $10 = 10^1$ The exponent "1" tell the number of times to multiply by 10 to get the original number.

$100 = 10^2$
$1000 = 10^3$
$10^0 = 1$

When the exponent is negative, it tells us how many times we need to *divide* by ten to get the original number.

For example, $0.025 = 2.5 \times 10$

The accepted format of scientific notation or writing numbers on their powers of 10 is $a \times 10^n$

Where a must be between 1 and 10, and n must be an integer.

How to Convert a Number To Scientific Notation

To convert a number to scientific notation, place a decimal after the first number that is not a zero, or, after the first number that between 1 and 9.

After placing the decimal, count the number of places the decimal had to move to get the exponent of 10. If the decimal moves to the left, then the exponent to multiply 10 will be in the positive. If the decimal moves from right to left, it will be a negative power of 10.

For example, to convert 29010, we need to place a decimal after 2, since 2 is the first non zero number. We would then have 2.91

If we were to convert 0.0167, we need to place the decimal after 1, since the first two numbers before 1 are zeros, and do not fall between 1 and 9. We would thus have 1.67

To complete the conversion of 29010 to scientific notation, we would get 2.91×10^4

The 10 is raised to the power of 4, because there are 4 places counting from right to left. This scientific notation is positive because the decimal moved to the left.

$0.0167 = 1.67 \times 10^{-2}$

In this example, the decimal place moved from left to right by 2 spaces thus the 10 is raised to the power of 2. It is negative, because the decimal moved to the right. How to convert from scientific notation

You may also need to convert numbers that are already represented in scientific notation or in their power of ten, to regular numbers.

First it is important to remember these two laws.

If the power is positive, shift decimal to the right
If the power is negative, shift decimal point to the left

Examples

Convert 3.201×10^3

This scientific notation is positive so shift the decimal to the right by 2 spaces, which is the power of the 10. We thus have: $3.201 \times 10^3 = 3201$

Another example

Convert
1.03×10^{-4}
The scientific notation here is negative and so we need to shift decimal to the left. Thus $1.03 \times 10^{-4} = 0.000103$ The decimal was shifted 4 spaces to the left.

Exponents and Radicals

Exponents: Tips, Short-cuts & Tricks

Exponents are just shorthand for saying that you're multiplying a number by itself two or more times.

For instance, instead of saying 5 x 5 x 5, you can show that you're multiplying 5 by itself 3 times if you just write 5^3.

We usually say this as "five to the third power" or "five to the power of three." In this example, the raised 3 is an "exponent," and the 5 is the "base."

You can even use exponents with fractions. For instance, $1/2^3$ means you're multiplying 1/2 x 1/2 x 1/2. (The answer is 1/8).

ACCUPLACER® Math Practice

https://youtu.be/NdjCVePr6ZM?si=Smb961yP1G3svBgv

Multiplying Exponents

For exponents with the same base, for instance $5^3 \times 5^2$, add the exponents and keep the same base. The answer, then, is 5^5.

If the bases are different, for example, in $5^3 \times 3^2$, you have to do the math the long way to figure it out.

5 x 5 x 5 = 125, and 3 X 3 = 9.

125 X 9 = 1125

Dividing Exponents

For exponents with the same base, subtract the exponents. In the problem above, $5^3 / 5^2$, 3 - 2 = 1. 5 to the power of 1 is 5.

Here are some Quick things to remember

Any number to the power of 1 is that number.

Any number raised to the power of 0 is 1.

Number (x)	x^2	x^3
1	1	1
2	4	8
3	9	27
4	16	64
5	25	125
6	36	216
7	49	343
8	64	512
9	81	729
10	100	1000
11	121	1331
12	144	1728
13	169	2197
14	196	2744
15	225	3375
16	256	4096

Simplifying Radicals

To simplify a radical (square root) Find the largest perfect square which will divide evenly into the number under the square root sign.

$\sqrt{60}$ - this can be re-written as $\sqrt{(3 * 16)}$

and then $3\sqrt{16}$

and

$\sqrt{128} = \sqrt{2}\sqrt{64} = 8\sqrt{2}$

Basic Math

Answer Sheet

	A	B	C	D	E		A	B	C	D	E
1	○	○	○	○	○	26	○	○	○	○	○
2	○	○	○	○	○	27	○	○	○	○	○
3	○	○	○	○	○	28	○	○	○	○	○
4	○	○	○	○	○	29	○	○	○	○	○
5	○	○	○	○	○	30	○	○	○	○	○
6	○	○	○	○	○	31	○	○	○	○	○
7	○	○	○	○	○	32	○	○	○	○	○
8	○	○	○	○	○	33	○	○	○	○	○
9	○	○	○	○	○	34	○	○	○	○	○
10	○	○	○	○	○	35	○	○	○	○	○
11	○	○	○	○	○	36	○	○	○	○	○
12	○	○	○	○	○	37	○	○	○	○	○
13	○	○	○	○	○	38	○	○	○	○	○
14	○	○	○	○	○	39	○	○	○	○	○
15	○	○	○	○	○	40	○	○	○	○	○
16	○	○	○	○	○	41	○	○	○	○	○
17	○	○	○	○	○	42	○	○	○	○	○
18	○	○	○	○	○	43	○	○	○	○	○
19	○	○	○	○	○	44	○	○	○	○	○
20	○	○	○	○	○	45	○	○	○	○	○
21	○	○	○	○	○	46	○	○	○	○	○
22	○	○	○	○	○	47	○	○	○	○	○
23	○	○	○	○	○	48	○	○	○	○	○
24	○	○	○	○	○	49	○	○	○	○	○
25	○	○	○	○	○	50	○	○	○	○	○

Basic Math Practice

1. 2/3 + 5/12 =

   a. 9/17`
   b. 3/11
   c. 7/12
   d. 1 1/12

2. 3/5 + 7/10 =

   a. 1 1/10
   b. 7/10
   c. 1 3/10
   d. 1 1/12

3. 4/5 – 2/3 =

   a. 2/2
   b. 2/13
   c. 1
   d. 2/15

4. 13/16 – 1/4 =

   a. 1
   b. 12/12
   c. 9/16
   d. 7/16

5. 15/16 x 8/9 =

    a. 5/6
    b. 16/37
    c. 2/11
    d. 5/7

6. 3/4 x 5/11 =

    a. 2/15
    b. 15/44
    c. 3/19
    d. 15/44

7. 5/8 ÷ 2/3 =

    a. 15/16
    b. 10/24
    c. 5/12
    d. 1 2/5

8. 2/15 ÷ 4/5 =

    a. 6/65
    b. 6/75
    c. 5/12
    d. 1/6

ACCUPLACER® Math Practice

9. In a class of 83 students, 72 are present. What percent of the students are absent? Provide answer up to two significant digits.

   a. 12%
   b. 13%
   c. 14%
   d. 15%

10. A woman spent 15% of her income on an item and ends with $120. What percentage of her income is left?

    a. 12%
    b. 85%
    c. 75%
    d. 95%

11. X% of 120 = 30. Solve for X.

    a. 15
    b. 12
    c. 4
    d. 25

12. Simplify 6 3/5 – 4 4/5

    a. 1 4/5
    b. 2 3/5
    c. 2 9/5
    d. 1 1/5

Basic Math

13. Express 25% as a fraction.

    a. 1/4
    b. 7/40
    c. 6/25
    d. 8/28

14. Express 125% as a decimal.

    a. .125
    b. 12.5
    c. 1.25
    d. 125

15. Express 24/56 as a reduced common fraction.

    a. 4/9
    b. 4/11
    c. 3/7
    d. 3/8

16. Express 71/1000 as a decimal.

    a. .71
    b. .0071
    c. .071
    d. 7.1

17. .4% of 36 is

    a. 1.44
    b. .144
    c. 14.4
    d. 144

18. Express 0.27 + 0.33 as a fraction.

    a. 3/6

    b. 4/7

    c. 3/5

    d. 2/7

19. 8 is what percent of 40?

    a. 10%

    b. 15%

    c. 20%

    d. 25%

20. 3.14 + 2.73 + 23.7 =

    a. 28.57

    b. 30.57

    c. 29.56

    d. 29.57

21. What is 1/3 of 3/4?

    a. 1/4

    b. 1/3

    c. 2/3

    d. 3/48

22. 15 is what percent of 200?

    a. 7.5%

    b. 15%

    c. 20%

    d. 17.50%

Basic Math

23. A boy has 5 red balls, 3 white balls and 2 yellow balls. What percent of the balls are yellow?

    a. 2%
    b. 8%
    c. 20%
    d. 12%

24. Add 10% of 300 to 50% of 20

    a. 50
    b. 40
    c. 60
    d. 45

25. Convert 75% to a fraction.

    a. 2/100
    b. 85/100
    c. 3/4
    d. 4/7

26. Multiply 3 by 25% of 40.

    a. 75
    b. 30
    c. 68
    d. 35

27. What is 10% of 30 multiplied by 75% of 200?

    a. 450
    b. 750
    c. 20
    d. 45

ACCUPLACER® Math Practice

28. Convert 4/20 to percent.

    a. 25%

    b. 20%

    c. 40%

    d. 30%

29. Write 765.3682 to the nearest 1000th.

    a. 765.368

    b. 765.36

    c. 765.3682

    d. 765.3

30. What number is in the ten thousandths place in 1.7389?

    a. 1

    b. 8

    c. 9

    d. 3

Scientific Notation

31. Convert 7,892,000,000 to scientific notation

    a. 7.892×10^{10}

    b. 7.892×10^{-9}

    c. 7.892×10^{9}

    d. 0.7892×10^{11}

— Basic Math —

32. Convert 0.045 to scientific notation

   a. 4.5×10^{-2}
   b. 4.5×10^{2}
   c. 4.05×10^{-2}
   d. 4.5×10^{-3}

33. Convert 20^{4} to scientific notation

   a. 2.04×10^{-2}
   b. 0.204×10^{2}
   c. 2.04×10^{3}
   d. 2.04×10^{2}

34. Convert 0.00002011 to scientific notation

   a. 2.011×10^{-4}
   b. 2.011×10^{5}
   c. 2.011×10^{-6}
   d. 2.011×10^{-5}

35. Convert 2.63×10^{-2} from scientific notation.

   a. 0.00263
   b. 0.0263
   c. 0.263
   d. 2.63

36. Convert 5.63×10^{6} from scientific notation.

   a. 5,630,000
   b. 563,000
   c. 5630
   d. 0.000005.630

Exponents and Radicals

37. Express in 3^4 standard form

   a. 81

   b. 27

   c. 12

   d. 9

38. Simplify $4^3 + 2^4$

   a. 45

   b. 108

   c. 80

   d. 48

39. If x = 2 and y = 5, solve $xy^3 - x^3$

   a. 240

   b. 258

   c. 248

   d. 242

40. $X^3 \times X^2$

   a. 5^x

   b. x^{-5}

   c. x^{-1}

   d. X^5

41. Divide 243 by 3^3

   a. 243
   b. 11
   c. 9
   d. 27

42. $7^5 - 3^5 =$

   a. 15,000
   b. 16,564
   c. 15,800
   d. 15,007

43. Solve for x if, 102 x 1002 = 1000x

   a. x = 2
   b. x = 3
   c. x = -2
   d. x = 0

44. Express 9 x 9 x 9 in exponential form and standard form.

   a. $9^3 = 719$
   b. $9^3 = 629$
   c. $9^3 = 729$
   d. $10^3 = 729$

45. Multiply 0.27 by 9^2

    a. 218.7

    b. 21.87

    c. 21

    d. 20.87

46. Solve $3^8/3^5$

    a. 3^3

    b. 3^5

    c. 3^6

    d. 3^4

47. Simply $\sqrt{27} * \sqrt{81}$

    a. $\sqrt{3^7}$

    b. $\sqrt{3^2}$

    c. $\sqrt{3^3}$

    d. $\sqrt{5^3}$

48. $\sqrt{8} * 3\sqrt{12}$

    a. $12\sqrt{3}$

    b. $3\sqrt{6}$

    c. $12\sqrt{6}$

    d. $8\sqrt{6}$

49. What is the result of the multiplication $(3 + \sqrt{5})^{120} * \sqrt{(14 - \sqrt{180})^{119}}$?

    a. $4^{59}(3 + \sqrt{5})$

    b. $2^{60}(3 - \sqrt{5})$

    c. $2^{119}(3 + 2\sqrt{5})$

    d. $2^{238}(3 + \sqrt{5})$

50. If $2^{x-1} = 3$, find the value of 8^x.

    a. 16

    b. 36

    c. 186

    d. 216

ACCUPLACER® Math Practice

Answer Key

1. D
A common denominator is needed, which both 3 and 12 will divide into. So, 8 + 5/12 = 13/12 = 1 1/12

2. C
A common denominator is needed for 5 and 10.
6 + 7/10 = 13/10 = 1 3/10

3. D
A common denominator is needed for 5 and 3.
12 - 10/15 = 2/15

4. C
A common denominator is needed for 16 and 4.
13 - 4/16 = 9/16

5. A
Since there are common numerators and denominators to cancel out, we cancel out 15/16 x 8/9 to get 5/2 x 1/3, and then multiply numerators and denominators to get 5/6

6. D
Since there are no common numerators and denominators to cancel out, we simply multiply the numerators and then the denominators. So 3 x 5/4 x 11 = 15/44

7. A
To divide fractions, multiply the first fraction with the inverse of the second. 5/8 x 3/2, = 15/16

8. D
Multiply the first fraction with the inverse of the second.
2/15 x 5/4, (cancel out) = 1/3 x 1/2 = 1/6

9. B
Number of absent students = 83 – 72 = 11
Percentage of absent students is found by proportioning the number of absent students to the total number of students in the class = 11 * 100/83 = 13.25

Checking the answer, round 13.25 to the nearest whole number: 13%.

10. B
Spent 15%, so 100% - 15% = 85%

11. D
X% of 120 = 30,
X/100 = 30/120
So X = 30/120 x 100/1
3000/120 = 300/12
X = 25

12. A
(6-4) (3/5 – 4/5) = 2 (3-4/5) = since 3 is less than 4, we would have to subtract 1 from the whole number besides the fraction, therefore 1 4/5

13. A
25% = 25/100 = 1/4

14. C
125/100 = 1.25

15. C
24/56 = 3/7 (divide numerator and denominator by 8)

16. C
Converting a fraction into a decimal – divide the numerator by the denominator – so 71/1000 = .071. Dividing by 1000 moves the decimal point 3 places to the left.

17. B
.4/100 * 36 = .4 * 36/100 = .144

ACCUPLACER® Math Practice

18. C
To convert a decimal to a fraction, take the places of decimal as your denominator, here, 2, so in 0.27, '7' is in the 100th place, so the fraction is 27/100 and 0.33 becomes 33/100.

Next estimate the answer quickly to eliminate obvious wrong choices. 27/100 is about 1/4 and 33/100 is 1/3. 1/3 is slightly larger than 1/4, and 1/4 + 1/4 is 1/2, so the answer will be slightly larger than 1/2.
Looking at the choices, Choice A can be eliminated since 3/6 = 1/2. Choice D, 2/7 is less than 1/2 and be eliminated. The answer is going to be Choice B or Choice C.

Do the calculation, 0.27 + 0.33 = 0.60 and 0.60 = 60/100 = 3/5, Choice C is correct.

19. C
This is an easy question, and shows how you can solve some questions without doing the calculations. The question is, 8 is what percent of 40. Take easy percentages for an approximate answer and see what you get.

10% is easy to calculate because you can drop the zero, or move the decimal point. 10% of 40 = 4, and 8 = 2 X 4, so, 8 must be 2 X 10% = 20%.

Here are the calculations which confirm the quick approximation.
8/40 = X/100 = 8 * 100 / 40X = 800/40 = X = 20

20. D
3.14 + 2.73 = 5.87 and 5.87 + 23.7 = 29.57

21. A
1/3 X 3/4 = 3/12 = 1/4
To multiply fractions, multiply the numerator and denominator.

22. A
15/200 = X/100
200X = (15 * 100)

— Basic Math —

1500/200 Cancel zeros in the numerator and denominator
15/2 = 7.5%.

Notice that the questions asks, What 15 is what percent of 200? The question does *not* ask, what is 15% of 200! The answers are very different.

23. C
Total no. of balls = 10, no. of yellow balls = 2, answer = 2/10 X 100 = 20%.

24. B
10% of 300 = 30 and 50% of 20 = 10 so 30 + 10 = 40.

25. C
75% = 75/100 = 3/4

26. B
25% of 40 = 10 and 10 x 3 = 30

27. A
10% of 30 = 3 and 75% of 200 = 150, 3 X 150 = 450

28. B
4/20 X 100 = 1/5 X 100 = 20%

29. A
The number is 51.738. The last digit, in the 1,000th place, 2, is less than 5, so it is discarded. Answer = 765.368.

30. C
9 is in the ten thousandths place in 1.7389, which is 4 places to the right of the decimal point.

Scientific Notation

31. C
The decimal moves 9 spaces left to be placed after 7, which is the first non-zero number. Thus 7.892×10^9

32. A
The decimal moves 2 spaces to the left to be placed before 4, which is the first non-zero number. 4.5×10^{-2} The answer is negative since the decimal moved left.

33. D
The decimal moves 2 spaces right to be placed after 2, which is the first non-zero number. 2.04×10^2

34. D
The decimal moves 5 places left to be placed after 2, which is the first non-zero number. 2.011×10^{-5} The answer is in negative because the decimal moved left.

35. B
The scientific notation is negative so we shift the decimal 2 places to the left. 0.0263

36. A
The scientific notation is in the positive so we shift the decimal 6 places to the right. 5,630,000

Exponents and Radicals

37. A
$3 \times 3 \times 3 \times 3 = 81$

38. C
$(4 \times 4 \times 4) + (2 \times 2 \times 2 \times 2) = 64 + 16 = 80$

39. D
$2(5)^3 - (2)^3 = 2(125) - 8 = 250 - 8 = 242$

40. D
$X^3 \times X^2 = X^{3+2} = X^5$

41. C

$243/3^3$ $3 \times 3 \times 3 = 27$
$243/27 = 9$

42. B
$(7 \times 7 \times 7 \times 7 \times 7) - (3 \times 3 \times 3 \times 3 \times 3) = 16,807 - 243 = 16,564$

43. A
$10 \times 10 \times 100 \times 100 = 1000^x$, $=100 \times 10,000 = 1000^x$, = $1,000,000 = 1000x = x = 2$

44. C
Exponential form is 9^3 and standard from is 729

45. B
$0.27 (9 \times 9) = 0.27 \times 81 = 21.87$

46. A
$3^{8-5} = 3^3$
To divide exponents with the same base, subtract the exponents.

47. A
$\sqrt{27} * \sqrt{81} = \sqrt{3^3} * \sqrt{3^4}$
$\sqrt{3^{3+4}} = \sqrt{3^7}$

48. C
$\sqrt{8} * 3\sqrt{12} = (\sqrt{2} * \sqrt{4}) * 3(\sqrt{4} * \sqrt{3})$
$= 2\sqrt{2} * ((3 * 2) * \sqrt{3})$
$= 2\sqrt{2} * 6 * \sqrt{3}$
$= 12 \sqrt{2} * \sqrt{3}$
$= 12 \sqrt{6}$

49. D
First, we need to simplify the term inside the root:
$\sqrt{180} = \sqrt{(62.5)} = 6\sqrt{5}$

$(3 + \sqrt{5})^{120} . \sqrt{(14 - \sqrt{180})^{119}} = (3 + \sqrt{5})^{120} * \sqrt{(14 - 6\sqrt{5})}119$
Notice that we need to find the way to simplify the second

term of the multiplication. $14 - 6\sqrt{5}$ is a perfect square:
$-6\sqrt{5} = -2ab$

$a = \sqrt{5}$ and $b = 3$

$14 = a^2 + b^2 = (\sqrt{5})^2 + 3^2$. So;

$(3 + \sqrt{5})120 * \sqrt{(14 - 6\sqrt{5})^{119}} = (3 + \sqrt{5})120 * \sqrt{((3 - \sqrt{5})2)^{119}}$

$= (3 + \sqrt{5})^{120} * (3 - \sqrt{5})2^{119} / 2$

$= (3 + \sqrt{5})^{120} * (3 - \sqrt{5})^{119}$

Remember that $(a - b)(a + b) = a^2 - b^2$:

$= (3 + \sqrt{5}) * (3 + \sqrt{5})^{119} * (3 - \sqrt{5})^{119}$
$= (3 + \sqrt{5}) * (3^2 - (\sqrt{5})2)^{119}$
$= (3 + \sqrt{5}) * 4^{119}$
$= 2^{238}(3 + \sqrt{5})$

50. D

In this question, we do not need to try to find the value of x. Notice that the numbers containing x as power are of base 2 both in the given and asked expressions. So, let us find the value of 2^x first:

$2^{x-1} = 3$

$2^{-1} * 2^x = 3$

$2^x = 3 * 2$

$2^x = 6$

The value of 8x is asked:

$8x = (2^3)^x = 2^{3x} = 6^3 = 216$

Translating the Text: Cracking Word Problems

Word problems are included in the Numerical Skills section of the Mathematics test.

Here is what you will learn:

Translate written scenarios into mathematical equations.

Identify "clue words" that indicate addition, subtraction, multiplication, or division.

Break down multi-step problems into manageable parts.

Draw diagrams to visualize complex problem statements.

Verify that your calculated answer makes sense in the real world.

How to Solve Word Problems

Do you know what the biggest tip for solving word problems is?

Practice regularly and systematically.

Sounds simple and easy right? Yes it is, and yes it really does work.

Word problems are a way of thinking and require you to translate a real-world problem into mathematical terms.

Some math teachers say that learning how to think mathematically is the main reason for teaching word problems.

So what does that mean?

Studying word problems and math in general requires a logical and mathematical frame of mind. The only way you can get this is by practicing regularly, which means every day.

It is critical that you practice word problems every day for the 5 days before the exam as the absolute minimum.

If you practice and miss a day, you have lost the mathematical frame of mind and the benefit of your previous practice is gone. You must start all over again.

Word Problems

Everything is important.

All the information given in the problem has some purpose. There is no unnecessary information! Word problems are typically around 50 words in 2 or 3 sentences.

Often, the relationships are complicated. To explain everything, every word counts.

Make sure that you use every piece of information.

9 steps to solving word problems

Step 1 – Read through the problem at least three times. The first reading should be a quick scan, and the next two readings should be done slowly to find answers to these important questions:

What does the problem ask? (Usually located towards the end of the problem)

What does the problem imply? (This is usually a point you were asked to remember).

Mark all information, and underline all important words or phrases.

Step 2 – Try to make a pictorial representation of the problem such as a circle and an arrow to show travel. This makes the problem a bit more real and sensible to you.

A favorite word problem is something like, 1 train leaves Station A traveling at 100 km/hr and another train leaves Station B traveling at 60 km/hr. ...

ACCUPLACER® Math Practice

Draw a line, the two stations, and the two trains at either end. This will help clarify the situation in your mind.

Step 3 – Use the information you have to make a table with a blank portion to show information you do not know.

Step 4 – Assign a single letter to represent each unknown data in your table. You can write down the unknown that each letter represents so that you do not make the error of assigning answers to the wrong unknown, because a word problem may have multiple unknowns and you will need to create equations for each unknown.

Step 5 – Translate the English terms in the word problem into a mathematical algebraic equation. Remember that the main problem with word problems is that they are not expressed in regular math equations. You ability to identify correctly the variables and translate the word problem into an equation determines your ability to solve the problem.

Step 6 – Check the equation to see if it looks like regular equations that you have seen before, and whether it looks sensible. Does the equation appear to represent the information in the question? Take note that you may need to rewrite some formulas needed to solve the word problem equation. For example, word distance problems may need rewriting the distance formula, which is Distance = Time x Rate. If the word problem requires that you solve for time you will need to use Distance/Rate and Distance/Time to solve for Rate. If you understand the distance word problem you should be able to identify the variable you need to solve for.

Step 7 – Use algebra rules to solve the derived equation. Take note that the laws of equation demands that what is done on this side of the equation has to also be done on the other side. You have to solve the equation so that the unknown ends up alone on one side. Where there are multiple unknowns you will need to use elimination or substitution methods to resolve all the equations.

Step 8 – Check your final answers to see if they make sense with the information given in the problem. For example if the word problem involves a discount, the final price should be less or if a product was taxed then the final answer has to cost more.

Step 9 – Cross check your answers by placing the answer or answers in the first equation to replace the unknown or unknowns. If your answer is correct then both side of the equation must equate or equal. If your answer is not correct then you may have derived a wrong equation or solved the equation wrongly. Repeat the necessary steps to correct.

Types of Word Problems

Word problems can be classified into 12 types. Below are examples of each type with a complete solution. Some types of word problems can be solved quickly using multiple choice strategies and some cannot. Always look for ways to estimate the answer and then eliminate choices.

1. Age

A girl is 10 years older than her brother. By next year, she will be twice the age of her brother. What are their ages now?

    a. 25, 15
    b. 19, 9
    c. 21, 11
    d. 29, 19

Solution: B

We will assume that the girl's age is "a" and her brother's age is "b." This means that based on the information in the first sentence,
a = 10 + b

Next year, she will be twice her brother's age, which gives, a + 1 = 2(b + 1)

We need to solve for one unknown factor and then use the answer to solve for the other. To do this we substitute the value of "a" from the first equation into the second equation. This gives

10+b + 1 = 2b + 2
11 + b = 2b + 2
11 − 2 = 2b − b
b= 9

9 = b this means that her brother is 9 years old. Solving for the girl's age in the first equation gives a = 10 + 9. a = 19 the girl is aged 19. So, the girl is aged 19 and the boy is 9

2. Distance or Speed

Two boats travel down a river towards the same destination, starting at the same time. One is traveling at 52 km/hr, and the other boat at 43 km/hr. How far apart will they be after 40 minutes?

    a. 46.67 km
    b. 19.23 km
    c. 6.4 km
    d. 14.39 km

Solution: C

After 40 minutes, the first boat will have traveled = 52 km/hr x 40 minutes/60 minutes = 34.7 km
After 40 minutes, the second boat will have traveled = 43 km/hr x 40/60 minutes = 28.66 km
Difference between the two boats will be 34.7 km – 28.66 km = 6.04 km.

Multiple Choice Strategy

First estimate the answer. The first boat is traveling 9 km. faster than the second, for 40 minutes, which is 2/3 of an hour. 2/3 of 9 = 6, as a rough guess of the distance apart.

Choices A, B and D can be eliminated right away.

3. Ratio

The instructions in a cookbook state that 700 grams of flour must be mixed in 100 ml of water, and 0.90 grams of salt added. A cook however has just 325 grams of flour. What is the quantity of water and salt that he should use?

    a. 0.41 grams and 46.4 ml
    b. 0.45 grams and 49.3 ml
    c. 0.39 grams and 39.8 ml
    d. 0.25 grams and 40.1 ml

Solution: A

The Cookbook states 700 grams of flour, but the cook only has 325. The first step is to determine the percentage of flour he has 325/700 x 100 = 46.4%
That means that 46.4% of all other items must also be used.
46.4% of 100 = 46.4 ml of water
46.4% of 0.90 = 0.41 grams of salt.

Multiple Choice Strategy

The recipe calls for 700 grams of flour but the cook only has 325, which is just less than half, the quantity of water and salt are going to be about half.

Choices C and D can be eliminated right away. Choice B is very close so be careful. Looking closely at choice B, it is exactly half, and since 325 is slightly less than half of 700, it can't be correct.

Choice A is correct.

4. Percent

An agent received $6,685 as his commission for selling a property. If his commission was 13% of the selling price, how much was the property?

    a. $68,825
    b. $121,850
    c. $49,025
    d. $51,423

Solution: D

Let's assume that the property price is x. That means from the information given, 13% of x = 6,685
Solve for x,

x = 6685 x 100/13 = $51,423

Multiple Choice Strategy

The commission, 13%, is just over 10%, which is easier to work with. Round up $6685 to $6700, and multiple by 10 for an approximate answer. 10 X 6700 = $67,000. You can do this in your head. Choice B is much too big and can be eliminated. Choice C is too small and can be eliminated. Choices A and D are left and good possibilities.

Do the calculations to make the final choice.

5. Sales & Profit

A store owner buys merchandise for $21,045. He transports them for $3,905 and pays his staff $1,450 to stock the merchandise on his shelves. If he does not incur further costs, how much does he need to sell the items to make $5,000 profit?

    a. $32,500
    b. $29,350
    c. $32,400
    d. $31,400

Solution: D

Total cost of the items is $21,045 + $3,905 + $1,450 = $26,400

Total cost is now $26,400 + $5000 profit = $31,400

Multiple Choice Strategy

Round off and add the numbers up in your head quickly. 21,000 + 4,000 + 1500 = 26500. Add in 5000 profit for a total of 31500.

Choice B is too small and can be eliminated. Choice C and Choice A are too large and can be eliminated.

6. Tax/Income

A woman earns $42,000 per month and pays 5% tax on her monthly income. If the Government increases her monthly taxes by $1,500, what is her income after tax?

    a. $38,400
    b. $36,050
    c. $40,500
    d. $39, 500

Solution: A

Initial tax on income was 5/100 x 42,000 = $2,100
$1,500 was added to the tax to give $2,100 + 1,500 = $3,600
Income after tax is $42,000 - $3,600 = $38,400

7. Simple Interest Word Problems

Simple interest is one type of interest problems. There are always four variables of any simple interest equation. With simple interest, you would be given three of these variables and be asked to solve for one unknown variable. With more complex interest problems, you would have to solve for multiple variables.

---Word Problems---

The four variables of simple interest are:

> P – Principal which refers to the original amount of money put in the account
> I – Interest or the amount of money earned as interest
> r – Rate or interest rate. This MUST ALWAYS be in decimal format and not in percentage
> t – Time or the amount of time the money is kept in the account to earn interest

The formula for simple interest is I = P x r x t

Example 1

A customer deposits $1,000 in a savings account with a bank that offers 2% interest. How much interest will be earned after 4 years?

For this problem, there are 3 variables as expected.

P = $1,000
t = 4 years
r = 2%
I = ?

Before we can begin solving for I using the simple interest formula, we need to first convert the rate from percentage to decimal.

2% = 2/100 = 0.02
Now we can use the formula: I = P x r x t

I = 1,000 x 0.02 x 4 = 80
This means that the $1,000 would have earned an interest of $80 after 4 years. The total in the account after 4 years will thus be principal + interest earned, or 1,000 + 80 = $1,080

ACCUPLACER® Math Practice

Example 2

Sandra deposits $1400 in a savings account with a bank at 5% interest. How long will she have to leave the money in the bank to earn $420 as interest to buy a second-hand car?

In this example, the given information is:
I = $420
P = $1,400
r - 5%
t - ?

As usual, first we convert the rate from percentage to decimal

5% = 5/100 = 0.05

Next, we plug in the variables we know into the simple interest formula - I = P x r x t

420 = 1,400 x 0.05 x t
420 = 70 x t
420 = 70t
t = 420/70
t = 6

Sandra will have to leave her $1,400 in the bank for 6 years to earn her an interest of $420 at a rate of 5%.

Other important simple interest formula to remember are below. To use these formula, do not convert r (rate) to decimal.

P = 100 x interest/ r x t
r = 100 x interest/p x t
t = 100 x interest/ p x r

―――― Word Problems ――――

8. Averaging

The average weight of 10 books is 54 grams. 2 more books were added and the average weight became 55.4. If one of the 2 new books added weighed 62.8 g, what is the weight of the other?

    a. 44.7 g
    b. 67.4 g
    c. 62 g
    d. 52 g

Solution: C

Total weight of 10 books with average 54 grams will be
= 10 × 54 = 540 g

Total weight of 12 books with average 55.4 will be
= 55.4 × 12 = 664.8 g

Total weight of the remaining 2 will be
= 664.8 − 540 = 124.8 g

If one weighs 62.8, the weight of the other will be
= 124.8 g − 62.8 g = 62 g

Multiple Choice Strategy

Averaging problems can be estimated by looking at which direction the average goes. If additional items are added and the average goes up, the new items much be greater than the average. If the average goes down after new items are added, the new items must be less than the average.

Here, the average is 54 grams and 2 books are added which increases the average to 55.4, so the new books must weight more than 54 grams.

Choices A and D can be eliminated right away.

9. Probability

A bag contains 15 marbles of various colors. If 3 marbles are white, 5 are red and the rest are black, what is the probability of randomly picking out a black marble from the bag?

    a. 7/15
    b. 3/15
    c. 1/5
    d. 4/15

Solution: A

Total marbles = 15
Number of black marbles = 15 − (3 + 5) = 7
Probability of picking out a black marble = 7/15

10. Two Variables

A company paid a total of $2850 to book for 6 single rooms and 4 double rooms in an hotel for one night. Another company paid $3185 to book for 13 single rooms for one night in the same hotel. What is the cost for single and double rooms in that hotel?

    a. single= $250 and double = $345
    b. single= $254 and double = $350
    c. single = $245 and double = $305
    d. single = $245 and double = $345

Solution: D

We can determine the price of single rooms from the information given of the second company. 13 single rooms = 3185.

One single room = 3185 / 13 = 245

The first company paid for 6 single rooms at $245. 245 x 6 = $1470

Total amount paid for 4 double rooms by first company = $2850 - $1470 = $1380

Cost per double room = 1380 / 4 = $345

11. Geometry

The length of a rectangle is 5 in. more than its width. The perimeter of the rectangle is 26 in. What is the width and length of the rectangle?

    a. width = 6 inches, Length = 9 inches
    b. width = 4 inches, Length = 9 inches
    c. width =4 inches, Length = 5 inches
    d. width = 6 inches, Length = 11 inches

Solution: B

Formula for perimeter of a rectangle is 2(L + W)
p = 26, so 2(L + W) = p

The length is 5 inches more than the width, so
2(w + 5) + 2w = 26
2w + 10 + 2w = 26
2w + 2w = 26 - 10
4w = 16

W = 16/4 = 4 inches

L is 5 inches more than w, so L = 5 + 4 = 9 inches.

12. Totals and fractions

A basket contains 125 oranges, mangoes and apples. If 3/5 of the fruits in the basket are mangoes and only 2/5 of the mangoes are ripe, how many ripe mangoes are there in the basket?

    a. 30
    b. 68
    c. 55
    d. 47

Solution: A

Number of mangoes in the basket is 3/5 x 125 = 75
Number of ripe mangoes = 2/5 x 75 = 30

Word Problem Practice with Video Solutions

HTTPS://YOUTU.BE/6XWA6FO6YCE

Most Common Word Problem Mistakes

Not reading the problem carefully and thoroughly, so that you either misunderstand or solve the problem incorrectly.

Not identifying the important information in the problem, such as the quantities, units, and the operation to be performed.

Not translating the information in the problem into mathematical language and equations.

Not checking the units of measure and making sure they match your final answer.

Not double-checking the answer to ensure it makes sense.

Not understanding the underlying mathematical concept or operation the problem is asking for.

Not using estimation or approximations as a tool to check the reasonableness of your answer.

ACCUPLACER® Math Practice

Answer Sheet

	A	B	C	D	E		A	B	C	D	E
1	○	○	○	○	○	21	○	○	○	○	○
2	○	○	○	○	○	22	○	○	○	○	○
3	○	○	○	○	○	23	○	○	○	○	○
4	○	○	○	○	○	24	○	○	○	○	○
5	○	○	○	○	○	25	○	○	○	○	○
6	○	○	○	○	○						
7	○	○	○	○	○						
8	○	○	○	○	○						
9	○	○	○	○	○						
10	○	○	○	○	○						
11	○	○	○	○	○						
12	○	○	○	○	○						
13	○	○	○	○	○						
14	○	○	○	○	○						
15	○	○	○	○	○						
16	○	○	○	○	○						
17	○	○	○	○	○						
18	○	○	○	○	○						
19	○	○	○	○	○						
20	○	○	○	○	○						

Word Problem Practice

1. Translate the following into an equation: Five greater than 3 times a number.

    a. 3X + 5
    b. 5X + 3
    c. (5 + 3)X
    d. 5(3 + X)

2. Translate the following into an equation: three plus a number times 7 equals 42.

    a. 7(3 + X) = 42
    b. 3(X + 7) = 42
    c. 3X + 7 = 42
    d. (3 + 7)X = 42

3. Translate the following into an equation: 2 + a number divided by 7.

    a. (2 + X)/7
    b. (7 + X)/2
    c. (2 + 7)/X
    d. 2/(7 + X)

4. Translate the following into an equation: six times a number plus five.

    a. 6X + 5
    b. 6(X+5)
    c. 5X + 6
    d. (6 * 5) + 5

ACCUPLACER® Math Practice

5. A box contains 7 black pencils and 28 blue ones. What is the ratio between the black and blue pens?

   a. 1:4
   b. 2:7
   c. 1:8
   d. 1:9

6. The manager of a weaving factory estimates that if 10 machines run at 100% efficiency for 8 hours, they will produce 1450 meters of cloth. Due to some technical problems, 4 machines run of 95% efficiency and the remaining 6 at 90% efficiency. How many meters of cloth can these machines will produce in 8 hours?

   a. 1334 meters
   b. 1310 meters
   c. 1300 meters
   d. 1285 meters

7. In a local election at polling station A, 945 voters cast their vote out of 1270 registered voters. At polling station B, 860 cast their vote out of 1050 registered voters and at station C, 1210 cast their vote out of 1440 registered voters. What is the total turnout from all three polling stations?

   a. 70%
   b. 74%
   c. 76%
   d. 80%

Word Problems

8. If Lynn can type a page in p minutes, what portion of the page can she do in 5 minutes?

    a. p/5
    b. p - 5
    c. p + 5
    d. 5/p

9. If Sally can paint a house in 4 hours, and John can paint the same house in 6 hours, how long will it take for both to paint a house?

    a. 2 hours and 24 minutes
    b. 3 hours and 12 minutes
    c. 3 hours and 44 minutes
    d. 4 hours and 10 minutes

10. Employees of a discount appliance store receive an additional 20% off the lowest price on any item. If an employee purchases a dishwasher during a 15% off sale, how much will he pay if the dishwasher originally cost $450?

    a. $280.90
    b. $287.00
    c. $292.50
    d. $306.00

11. The sale price of a car is $12,590, which is 20% off the original price. What is the original price?

    a. $14,310.40
    b. $14,990.90
    c. $15,108.00
    d. $15,737.50

12. Richard gives 's' amount of salary to each of his 'n' employees weekly. If he has 'x' amount of money, how many days he can employ these 'n' employees.

    a. sx/7n

    b. 7x/nx

    c. nx/7s

    d. 7x/ns

13. A distributor purchased 550 pounds of potatoes for $165. He distributed these at a rate of $6.4 per 20 pounds to 15 shops, $3.4 per 10 pounds to 12 shops and the remainder at $1.8 per 5 pounds. If his total distribution cost is $10, what will his profit be?

    a. $10.40

    b. $8.60

    c. $14.90

    d. $23.40

14. How much pay does Mr. Johnson receive if he gives half of his pay to his family, $250 to his landlord, and has exactly 3/7 of his pay left over?

    a. $3600

    b. $3500

    c. $2800

    d. $1750

── Word Problems ──

15. The cost of waterproofing canvas is .50 a square yard. What's the total cost for waterproofing a canvas truck cover that is 15' x 24'?

    a. $18.00
    b. $6.67
    c. $180.00
    d. $20.00

16. The price of a book went from $20 to $25. What percent did the price increase?

    a. 5%
    b. 10%
    c. 20%
    d. 25%

17. In the time required to serve 43 customers, a server breaks 2 glasses and slips 5 times. The next day, the same server breaks 10 glasses. Assuming that glasses broken is proportional to customers served, how many customers did she serve?

    a. 25
    b. 43
    c. 86
    d. 215

ACCUPLACER® Math Practice

18. A square lawn has an area of 62,500 square meters. What is the cost of building fence around it at a rate of $5.5 per meter?

   a. $4000
   b. $4500
   c. $5000
   d. $5500

19. Susan wants to buy a leather jacket that costs $545.00 and is on sale for 10% off. What is the approximate cost?

   a. $525
   b. $450
   c. $475
   d. $500

20. Sarah weighs 25 pounds more than Tony. If together they weigh 205 pounds, how much does Sarah weigh in kilograms? Assume 1 pound = 0.4535 kilograms.

   a. 41
   b. 48
   c. 50
   d. 52

―――― Word Problems ――――

21. A man buys an item for $420 and has a balance of $3000.00. How much did he have before his purchase?

    a. $2,580
    b. $3,420
    c. $2,420
    d. $342

22. The average weight of 13 students in a class of 15 (two were absent that day) is 42 kg. When the remaining two are weighed, the average became 42.7 kg. If one of the remaining students weighs 48 kg., how much does the other weigh?

    a. 44.7 kg.
    b. 45.6 kg.
    c. 46.5 kg.
    d. 47.4 kg.

23. The total expense of building a fence around a square-shaped field is $2000 at a rate of $5 per meter. What is the length of one side?

    a. 40 meters
    b. 80 meters
    c. 100 meters
    d. 320 meters

24. There were some oranges in a basket. By adding 8/5 of the total to the basket, the new total is 130. How many oranges were in the basket?

    a. 60

    b. 50

    c. 40

    d. 35

25. A person earns $25,000 per month and pays $9,000 income tax per year. The Government increased income tax by 0.5% per month and his monthly earning was increased $11,000. How much more income tax will he pay per month?

    a. $1260

    b. $1050

    c. $750

    d. $510

Answer Key

Part 1 - Equation Translation

1. A
Five greater than 3 times a number.
5 + 3 times a number.
3X + 5

2. A
Three plus a number times 7 equals 42.
Let X be the number.
(3 + X) times 7 = 42
7(3 + X) = 42

3. A
2 + a number divided by 7.
(2 + X) divided by 7.
(2 + X)/7

4. B
Six times a number plus five is the same as saying six times (a number plus five). Or,
6 * (a number plus five). Let X be the number so,
6(X + 5).

5. A
The ratio between black and blue pens is 7 to 28 or 7:28. Bring to the lowest terms by dividing both sides by 7 gives 1:4.

6. A
At 100% efficiency 1 machine produces 1450/10 = 145 m of cloth.

At 95% efficiency, 4 machines produce 4 * 145 * 95/100 = 551 m of cloth.

At 90% efficiency, 6 machines produce 6 * 145 * 90/100 = 783 m of cloth.

Total cloth produced by all 10 machines = 551 + 783 = 1334 m

Since the information provided and the question are based on 8 hours, we did not need to use time to reach the answer.

7. D

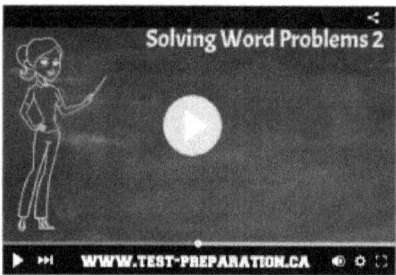

https://youtu.be/Es3Yg5pfYeY

To find the total turnout in all three polling stations, we need to proportion the number of voters to the number of all registered voters.

Number of total voters = 945 + 860 + 1210 = 3015

Number of total registered voters = 1270 + 1050 + 1440 = 3760

Percentage turnout over all three polling stations = 3015 * 100/3760 = 80.19%

Checking the answers, we round 80.19 to the nearest whole number: 80%

8. D

https://youtu.be/syDAMxmkYgY

ACCUPLACER® Math Practice

This is a simple direct proportion problem:
If Lynn can type 1 page in p minutes,

   she can type x pages in 5 minutes

We do cross multiplication: x * p = 5 * 1

Then,

x = 5/p

9. A
This is an inverse ratio problem.

1/x = 1/a + 1/b where a is the time Sally can paint a house, b is the time John can paint a house, x is the time Sally and John can together paint a house.

So,

1/x = 1/4 + 1/6 ... We use the least common multiple in the denominator that is 24:

1/x = 6/24 + 4/24

1/x = 10/24

x = 24/10

x = 2.4 hours.

In other words; 2 hours + 0.4 hours = 2 hours + 0.4•60 minutes

= 2 hours 24 minutes

10. D

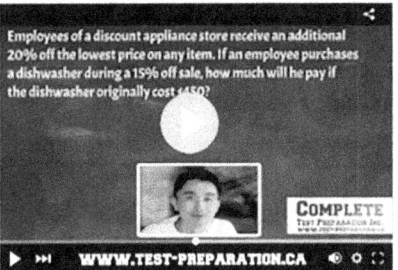

https://youtu.be/l_FaJPJzepE

The cost of the dishwasher = $450

15% discount amount = 450•15/100 = $67.5

The discounted price = 450 − 67.5 = $382.5

20% additional discount amount on lowest price = 382.5•20/100 = $76.5

So, the final discounted price = 382.5 - 76.5 = $306.00

11. D
Original price = x,
80/100 = 12590/X,
80X = 1259000,
X = 15,737.50.

12. D

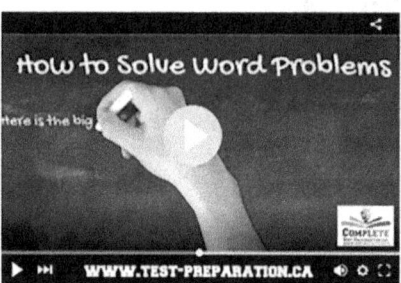

https://youtu.be/EF92e6V4mAA

We are given that each of the n employees earns s amount of salary weekly. This means that one employee earns s salary weekly. So; Richard has 'ns' amount of money to employ n employees for a week.
We are asked to find the number of days n employees can be employed with x amount of money. We can do

simple direct proportion:

If Richard can employ n employees for 7 days with 'ns' amount of money,

Richard can employ n employees for y days with x amount of money ... y is the number of days we need to find.

We can cross multiply:

y = (x * 7)/(ns)

y = 7x/ns

13. B
The distribution is done at three different rates and in three different amounts:

$6.4 per 20 kilograms to 15 shops ... 20•15 = 300 kilograms distributed

$3.4 per 10 kilograms to 12 shops ... 10•12 = 120 kilograms distributed

550 - (300 + 120) = 550 - 420 = 130 kilograms left. This amount is distributed in 5 kilogram portions. So, this means that there are 130/5 = 26 shops.

$1.8 per 130 kilograms.

We need to find the amount he earned overall these distributions.

$6.4 per 20 kilograms : 6.4 * 15 = $96 for 300 kilograms

$3.4 per 10 kilograms : 3.4 *12 = $40.8 for 120 kilograms

$1.8 per 5 kilograms : 1.8 * 26 = $46.8 for 130 kilograms

So, he earned 96 + 40.8 + 46.8 = $ 183.6

The total distribution cost is given as $10

The profit is found by: Money earned - money spent ... It is important to remember that he bought 550 kilograms of potatoes for $165 at the beginning:

Profit = 183.6 - 10 - 165 = $8.6

14. B
We check the fractions taking place in the question. We see that there is a "half" (that is 1/2) and 3/7. So, we multiply the denominators of these fractions to decide how to name the total money. We say that Mr. Johnson has 14x at the beginning; he gives half of this, meaning 7x, to his family. $250 to his landlord. He has 3/7 of his money left. 3/7 of 14x is equal to:

14x * (3/7) = 6x

So,

Spent money is: 7x + 250

Unspent money is: 6x

Total money is: 14x

Write an equation: total money = spent money + unspent money

14x = 7x + 250 + 6x

14x - 7x - 6x = 250

x = 250

We are asked to find the total money that is 14x:

14x = 14 * 250 = $3500

15. D
First calculate total square feet, which is 15•24 = 360 ft2. Next, convert this value to square yards, (1 yards2 = 9 ft2) which is 360/9 = 40 yards2. At $0.50 per square yard, the total cost is 40 * 0.50 = $20.

16. D
Price increased by $5 ($25-$20). To calculate the percent increase:
5/20 = X/100
500 = 20X
X = 500/20
X = 25%

17. D
2 glasses are broken for 43 customers so 1 glass breaks for every 43/2 customers served, therefore 10 glasses implies (43/2) * 10 = 215 customers.

18. D
As the lawn is square, the length of one side will be the square root of the area. $\sqrt{62,500}$ = 250 meters. So, the perimeter is found by 4 times the length of the side of the square:

250 * 4 = 1000 meters.

Since each meter costs $5.5, the total cost of the fence will be 1000 * 5.5 = $5,500.

19. D
The question asks for approximate cost, so work with round numbers. The jacket costs $545.00 so we can round up to $550. 10% of $550 is 55. We can round down to $50, which is easier to work with. $550 - $50 is $500. The jacket will cost about $500.
The actual cost will be 10% X 545 = $54.50
545 – 54.50 = $490.50

ACCUPLACER® Math Practice

20. D

Let us denote Sarah's weight by "x." Then, since she weighs 25 pounds more than Tony, so he will be x - 25. They together weigh 205 pounds which means that the sum of the two representations will be equal to 205:

Sarah : x

Tony : x - 25

x + (x - 25) = 205 ... by arranging this equation we have:

x + x - 25 = 205

2x - 25 = 205 ... we add 25 to each side to have x term alone:

2x - 25 + 25 = 205 + 25

2x = 230

x = 230/2

x = 115 pounds → Sarah weighs 115 pounds. Since 1 pound is 0.4535 kilograms, we need to multiply 115 by 0.4535 to have her weight in kilograms:

x = 115 * 0.4535 = 52.1525 kilograms → this is equal to 52 when rounded to the nearest whole number.

21. B

(Amount Spent) $420 + $3000 (Balance) = $3,420.00

22. C

Total weight of 13 students with average 42 will be = 42 * 13 = 546 kg.

The total weight of the remaining 2 will be found by subtracting the total weight of 13 students from the total weight of 15 students: 640.5 - 546 = 94.5 kg.

94.5 = the total weight of two students. One of these students weigh 48 kg, so;

The weight of the other will be = 94.5 – 48 = 46.5 kg

23. C
Total expense is $2000 and we are informed that $5 is spent per meter. Combining these two information, we know that the total length of the fence is 2000/5 = 400 meters.

The fence is built around a square field. If one side of the square is "a," the perimeter of the square is "4a." Here, the perimeter is equal to 400 meters. So,

400 = 4a

100 = a → this means that one side of the square is equal to 100 meters

24. B
Let the number of oranges in the basket before additions = x
Then: X + 8x/5 = 130
5x + 8x = 650
650 = 13x
X = 50

25. D
The income tax per year is $9,000. So, the income tax per month is 9,000/12 = $750.

This person earns $25,000 per month and pays $750 income tax. We need to find the rate of the income tax:

Tax rate: 750 * 100/25,000 = 3%
Government increased this rate by 0.5% so it became 3.5%.

The income of the person per month is increased

$11,000 so it became:

$25,000 + $11,000 = $36,000.

The new monthly income tax is: 36,000 * 3.5/100 = $1260.

Amount of increase in tax per month is:
$1260 - $750 = $510.

X = 50

25. D
The income tax per year is $9,000. So, the income tax per month is 9,000/12 = $750.

This person earns $25,000 per month and pays $750 income tax. We need to find the rate of the income tax:

Tax rate: 750 * 100/25,000 = 3%
Government increased this rate by 0.5% so it became 3.5%.

The income of the person per month is increased $11,000 so it became:

$25,000 + $11,000 = $36,000.

The new monthly income tax is: 36,000 * 3.5/100 = $1260.

Amount of increase in tax per month is:
$1260 - $750 = $510.

Shapes and Space: Navigating Geometry

Geometry

Geometry

THE BASIC GEOMETRY SECTION INCLUDES:

- slope of a line
- Identify linear equations from a graph
- Calculate perimeter, circumference and volume
- Solve problems using the Pythagorean theorem
- Determine geometric transformations
- Solve real world problems using the properties of geometric shapes

Cartesian Plane, Coordinate Grid and Plane

To locate points and draw lines and curves, we use the coordinate plane. It also called Cartesian coordinate plane. It is a two-dimensional surface with a coordinate grid in it, which helps us to count the units. For the counting of those units, we use x-axis (horizontal scale) and y-axis (vertical scale).

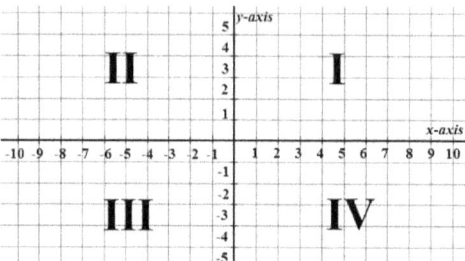

The whole system is called a coordinate system which is divided into 4 parts, called quadrants. The quadrant where all numbers are positive is the 1st quadrant (I), and if we go counterclockwise, we mark all 4 quadrants.

The location of a dot in the coordinate system is represented by coordinates. Coordinates are represented as a pair of numbers, where the 1st number is located on the x-axis and the 2nd number is located on the y-axis. So, if a dot A has coordinates a and b, then we write:

A=(a,b) or A(a,b)

The point where x-axis and y-axis intersect is called an origin. The origin is the point from which we measure the distance along the x and y axes.

In the Cartesian coordinate system we can calculate the distance between 2 given points. If we have dots with coordinates:
A=(a,b)
B=(c,d)

Then the distance d between A and B can be calculated by the following formula:

$$d = \sqrt{(c-a)^2 + (d-b)^2}$$

Cartesian coordinate system is used for the drawing of 2-dimentional shapes, and is also commonly used for functions.

Example:

Draw the function y = (1 - x)/2

To draw a linear function, we need at least 2 points. If we put that x=0 then value for y would be:

$$y = \frac{1-x}{2} = \frac{1-0}{2} = \frac{1}{2}$$

We found the 1st point, let's name it A, with following coordinates:

A = (0,1/2)

To find the 2nd point, we can put that x=1. Here, the value for y would be:

$$y = \frac{1-x}{2} = \frac{1-1}{2} = \frac{0}{2} = 0$$

If we denote the 2nd point with B, then the coordinates for this point are:

B=(1,0)

Since we have 2 points necessary for the function, we find them in the coordinate system and we connect them with a line that represents the function,

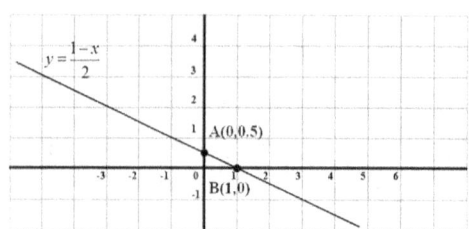

Perimeter Area and Volume

Perimeter and Area (2-dimentional shapes)

Perimeter of a shape determines the length around that shape, while the area includes the space inside the shape.

Rectangle:

$P = 2a + 2b$
$A = ab$

Square

$P = 4a$
$A = a^2$

Parallelogram

$P = 2a + 2b$
$A = ah_a = bh_b$

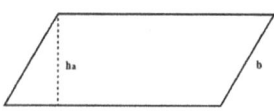

Rhombus

$P = 4a$

$A = ah = \dfrac{d_1 d_2}{2}$

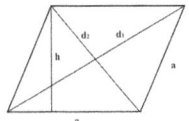

Triangle

$P = a + b + c$

$A = \dfrac{a h_a}{2} = \dfrac{b h_b}{2} = \dfrac{c h_c}{2}$

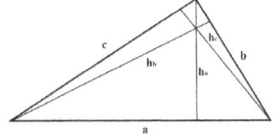

Equilateral Triangle

$P = 3a$

$A = \dfrac{a^2 \sqrt{3}}{4}$

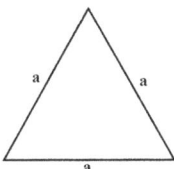

Trapezoid

$P = a + b + c + d$

$A = \dfrac{a+b}{2} h$

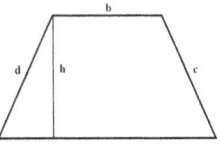

Circle

$P = 2r\pi$

$A = r^2 \pi$

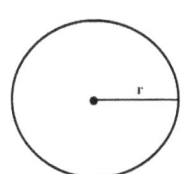

Area and Volume (3-dimentional shapes)

To calculate the area of a 3-dimentional shape, we calculate the areas of all sides and then we add them all.

To find the volume of a 3-dimentional shape, we multiply the area of the base (B) and the height (H) of the 3-dimentional shape.

$$V = BH$$

In case of a pyramid and a cone, the volume would be divided by 3.

$$V = BH/3$$

Here are some of the 3-dimentional shapes with formulas for their area and volume:

Cuboids

$A = 2(ab + bc + ac)$
$V = abc$

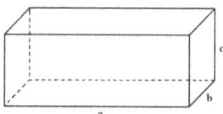

Cube

$A = 6a^2$
$V = a^3$

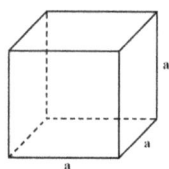

Basic Geometry

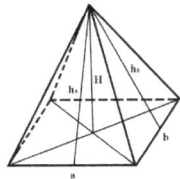

Pyramid

$A = ab + ah_a + bh_b$

$V = \dfrac{abH}{3}$

Cylinder

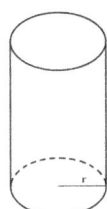

$A = 2r^2\pi + 2r\pi H$

$V = r^2\pi H$

Cone

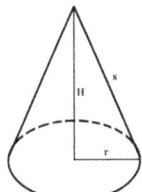

$A = (r+s)r\pi$

$V = \dfrac{r^2\pi H}{3}$

Pythagorean Geometry

If we have a right triangle ABC, where its sides (legs) are a and b and c is a hypotenuse (the side opposite the right angle), then we can establish a relationship between these sides using the following formula:

$c^2 = a^2 + b^2$

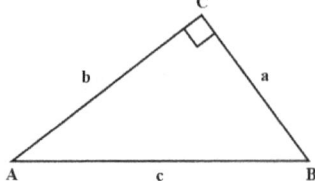

This formula is proven in the Pythagorean Theorem. There are many proofs of this theorem, but we'll look at just one geometrical proof:

If we draw squares on the right triangle's sides, then the area of the square upon the hypotenuse is equal to the sum of the areas of the squares that are upon other two sides of the triangle. Since the areas of these squares are a², b² and c², that is how we got the formula above.

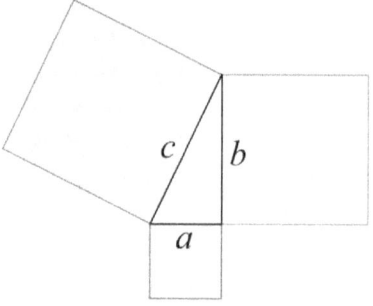

One of the famous right triangles is one with sides 3, 4 and 5. And we can see here that:

3² + 4² = 5²
9 + 16 = 25
25 = 25

Example Problem:

The isosceles triangle ABC has a perimeter of 18 centimeters, and the difference between its base and legs is 3 centimeters. Find the height of this triangle.

We write the information we have about triangle ABC and we draw a picture for a better understanding of the rela-

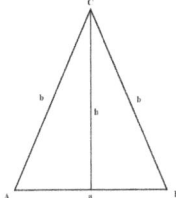

tion between its elements:
P = 18 cm
a - b = 3 cm
h = ?

We use the formula for the perimeter of the isosceles triangle, since that is what is given to us:
P = a + 2b = 18 cm

Notice that we have 2 equations with 2 variables, so we can solve it as a system of equations:

a + 2b = 18
a − b = 3 / a + 2b = 18
2a - 2b = 6 / a + 2b + 2a - 2b = 18 + 6
3a = 24
a = 24/3 = 8 cm

Now we go back to find b:
a - b = 3
8 - b = 3
b = 8 - 3
b = 5 cm

Using Pythagorean Theorem, we can find the height using a and b, because the height falls on the side a at the right angle. Notice that height cuts side a exactly in half, and that's why we use in the formula a/2. Here, b is our hypotenuse, so we have:

$b^2 = (a/2)^2 + h^2$
$h^2 = b^2 - (a/2)^2$
$h^2 = 5^2 - (8/2)^2$
$h^2 = 5^2 - (8/2)^2$
$h^2 = 25 - 4^2$
$h^2 = 26 - 16$
$h^2 = 9$
$h = 3$ cm.

Quadrilaterals

Quadrilaterals are 2-dimentional geometrical shapes that have 4 sides and 4 angles. There are many types of quadrilaterals, depending on the length of its sides, if they are parallel, and the size of its angles. All quadrilaterals have the following properties:

Sum of all interior angles is 360°

Sum of all exterior angles is 360°

A quadrilateral is a parallelogram is it fulfills at least one of the following conditions:

- Angles on each side are supplementary
- Opposite angles are equal
- Opposite sides are equal
- Diagonals intersect each other exactly in half

Basic Geometry

Here are some of the quadrilaterals:

Square

All sides are equal
All angles are right angles

Rectangle

2 pairs of equal sides
All angles are right angles

Parallelogram

2 pairs of equal sides
Opposite angles are equal

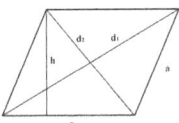

Rhombus

All sides are equal
Opposite angles are equal

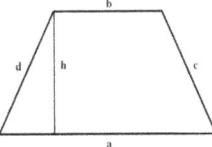

Trapezoid

One pair of parallel sides

Example Problem
Find all angles of a parallelogram if one angle is greater than the other one by 40°.

First, we draw an image of a parallelogram:

We denote angles by α and β, Since this is a parallelogram, the opposite angles are equal.

We are given that one angle is greater than the other one by 40°, so we can write:

β = α + 40°

We solve this problem in two ways:
1) The sum of all internal angles of every quadrilateral is 360°. There are 2 α and 2 β. So we have:
2α + 2β = 360°
Now, instead of β we write α + 40:
2 α + 2 (α + 40°) =360°
2 α + 2 α + 80° = 360°
4 α = 360° - 80°
4 α = 280°
α = 280° / 4
α = 70°
Now we can find β from α:
β = α + 40°
β = 70° + 40°
β = 110°

2) One condition for parallelogram is " Angles on each side are supplementary" and we can use that to find these angles:
α + β = 180°
α + α + 40°= 180°
2 α = 180°- 40°

$2\alpha = 140°$
$\alpha = 70°$

Now we find β:
$\beta = \alpha + 40°$
$\beta = 70° + 40°$
$\beta = 110°$

Geometric Transformations

If we want to move a geometric shape, or change its direction or size, we would use one of the following geometric transformations:

1) Dilation
2) Translation
3) Rotation
4) Reflection

Dilation

Dilation is transformation where 2D shape is either enlarged or contracted, where the direction of the shape is kept. If we have a triangle ABC that we want to reduce to a new triangle half of its size, we would make an arbitrary point of dilation O and connect it with points A, B and C. We find the centers of lines OA, OB and OC and mark them as A', B' and C', respectively. We cut the lines in half because we want the new triangle to be half the size of the original one. These new points make the triangle A'B'C' which is the one we are looking for.

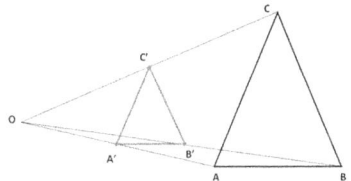

Translation

Translation is a transformation we use for moving the 2D shapes, without changing their size or direction. It can be moved using a grid or a coordinate system. If we have a square ABCD in a grid we want to move 6 units to the left and 5 units down, we move each point of the square and we connect the new points, where we get a new square A'B'C'D' with exactly same size and direction.

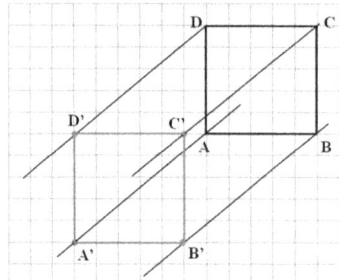

Rotation

Rotation is a transformation where we only change the direction of a 2D shape, but not the size. We make an arbitrary center of the rotation O, and if we want to rotate a triangle ABC by, for example, 45°, then we rotate every point of the triangle by 45°, where we have that OA is equal to OA', and same goes for OB and OC. The triangle A'B'C' is actually triangle ABC rotated by 45°.

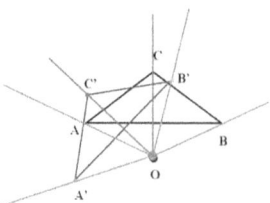

Basic Geometry

Reflection

Reflection is a transformation where we make a mirror image of some 2D shape. Reflection changes the direction of the shape, but not its size. We are given a mirror line p which we use to reflect each point of the shape doing this: we make a line through each point of the shape, in this case of the triangle ABC, and these lines should intersect the mirror line p at right angle, we then measure the distance from the intersection and the original point and we find the mirror point using that distance. We connect mirror points and we get a reflected triangle A'B'C'.

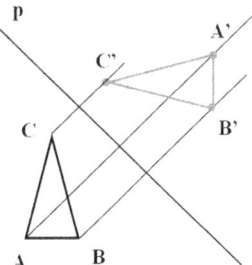

Example:

Reflect the square ABCD with the given mirror line p.

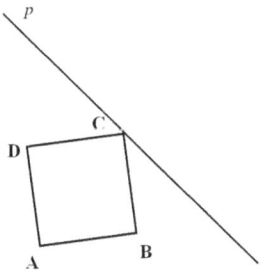

Since the point C is already on the mirror line, we don't have to reflect it. From points A, B and D we draw the lines that intersect with the mirror line at right angle. We measure the distance from the mirror line to the A, B and D and we use those distance to find points A', B' and D', respectively, on the same line on the other side of the mirror line.

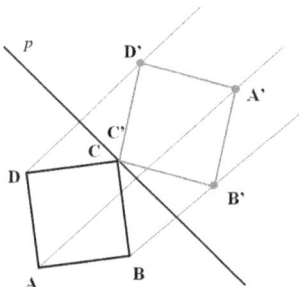

Example 2

Let's reflect triangle ABC against the mirror line m that are given in the picture.

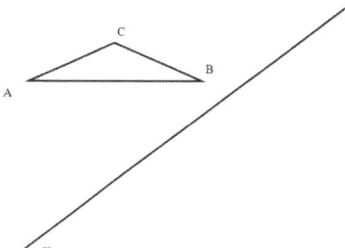

We draw lines from each point of the triangle ABC which will intersect with the mirror line at the right angle. We measure the distance from the triangle's points to the line m, and we use them to find points A', B' and C'. We connect the new points and we get a reflection of the triangle ABC, that is triangle A'B'C'.

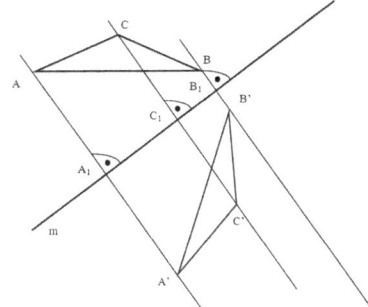

What if we have a geometrical shape that intersects with the mirror line, such as line AB below?

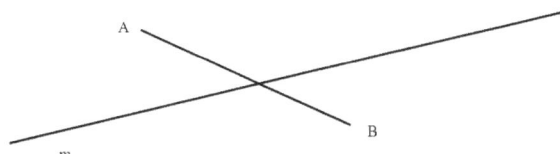

We reflect points A and B, no matter if they are on the different sides of the mirror line.

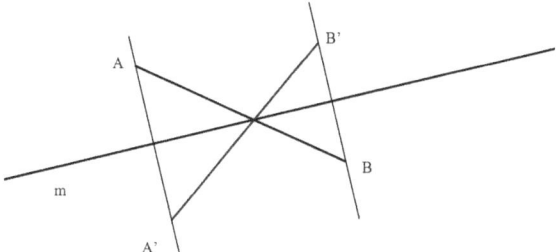

ACCUPLACER® Math Practice

Answer Sheet

1. Ⓐ Ⓑ Ⓒ Ⓓ   21. Ⓐ Ⓑ Ⓒ Ⓓ
2. Ⓐ Ⓑ Ⓒ Ⓓ   22. Ⓐ Ⓑ Ⓒ Ⓓ
3. Ⓐ Ⓑ Ⓒ Ⓓ   23. Ⓐ Ⓑ Ⓒ Ⓓ
4. Ⓐ Ⓑ Ⓒ Ⓓ   24. Ⓐ Ⓑ Ⓒ Ⓓ
5. Ⓐ Ⓑ Ⓒ Ⓓ   25. Ⓐ Ⓑ Ⓒ Ⓓ
6. Ⓐ Ⓑ Ⓒ Ⓓ   26. Ⓐ Ⓑ Ⓒ Ⓓ
7. Ⓐ Ⓑ Ⓒ Ⓓ   27. Ⓐ Ⓑ Ⓒ Ⓓ
8. Ⓐ Ⓑ Ⓒ Ⓓ   28. Ⓐ Ⓑ Ⓒ Ⓓ
9. Ⓐ Ⓑ Ⓒ Ⓓ   29. Ⓐ Ⓑ Ⓒ Ⓓ
10. Ⓐ Ⓑ Ⓒ Ⓓ   30. Ⓐ Ⓑ Ⓒ Ⓓ
11. Ⓐ Ⓑ Ⓒ Ⓓ   31. Ⓐ Ⓑ Ⓒ Ⓓ
12. Ⓐ Ⓑ Ⓒ Ⓓ   32. Ⓐ Ⓑ Ⓒ Ⓓ
13. Ⓐ Ⓑ Ⓒ Ⓓ   33. Ⓐ Ⓑ Ⓒ Ⓓ
14. Ⓐ Ⓑ Ⓒ Ⓓ   34. Ⓐ Ⓑ Ⓒ Ⓓ
15. Ⓐ Ⓑ Ⓒ Ⓓ   35. Ⓐ Ⓑ Ⓒ Ⓓ
16. Ⓐ Ⓑ Ⓒ Ⓓ   36. Ⓐ Ⓑ Ⓒ Ⓓ
17. Ⓐ Ⓑ Ⓒ Ⓓ   37. Ⓐ Ⓑ Ⓒ Ⓓ
18. Ⓐ Ⓑ Ⓒ Ⓓ   38. Ⓐ Ⓑ Ⓒ Ⓓ
19. Ⓐ Ⓑ Ⓒ Ⓓ   39. Ⓐ Ⓑ Ⓒ Ⓓ
20. Ⓐ Ⓑ Ⓒ Ⓓ   40. Ⓐ Ⓑ Ⓒ Ⓓ

Basic Geometry

Geometry Practice Questions

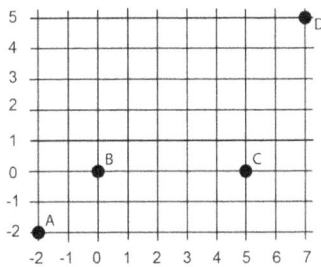

1. Which of the above points represents the origin?

   a. A
   b. B
   c. C
   d. D

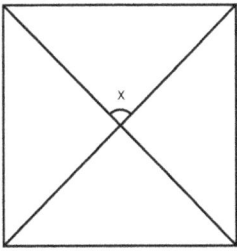

2. What is measurement of the indicated angle?

   a. 45°
   b. 90°
   c. 60°
   d. 30°

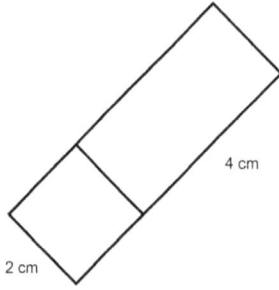

Note: figure not drawn to scale.

3. Assuming the figure with side 2 cm. is square, what is the perimeter of the above shape?

    a.   12 cm
    b.   16 cm
    c.   6 cm
    d.   20 cm

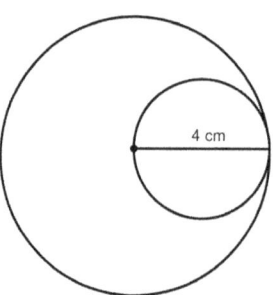

Note: Figure not drawn to scale

--- Basic Geometry ---

4. Assuming the diameter of the small circle is the radius of the larger circle, what is (area of large circle) - (area of small circle) in the figure above?

   a. 8 π cm²
   b. 10 π cm²
   c. 12 π cm²
   d. 16 π cm²

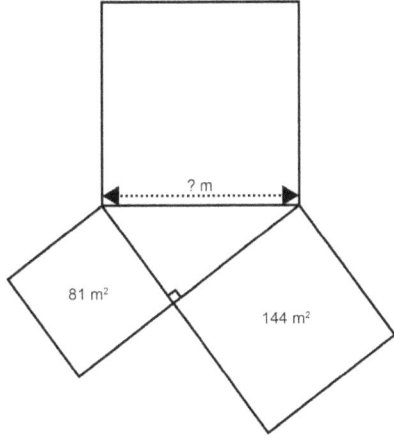

Note: Figure not drawn to scale

5. Assuming the shapes around the center right triangle are square, what is the length of each side of the indicated square above?

   a. 10
   b. 15
   c. 20
   d. 5

6. Choose the expression the figure represents.

    a. $X \leq 1$
    b. $X < 1$
    c. $X > 1$
    d. $X \geq 1$

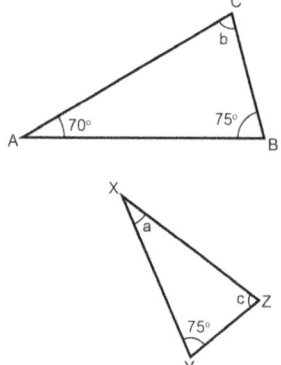

7. What are the respective values of a, b & c if both triangles are similar?

    a. 70°, 70°, 35°
    b. 70°, 35°, 70°
    c. 35°, 35°, 35°
    d. 70°, 75°, 35°

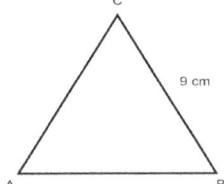

Note: figure not drawn to scale

8. What is the perimeter of the equilateral △ABC above?

    a. 18 cm
    b. 12 cm
    c. 27 cm
    d. 15 cm

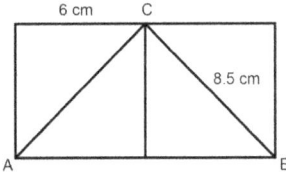

Note: figure not drawn to scale

9. Assuming the 2 quadrangles are identical rectangles, what is perimeter of △ABC in the above shape?

    a. 25.5 cm
    b. 27 cm
    c. 30 cm
    d. 29 cm

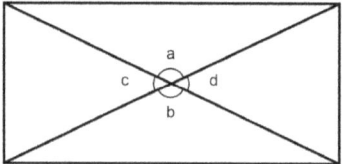

10. What is the sum of the angles in the rectangle above?

    a. 180°
    b. 360°
    c. 90°
    d. 120°

Note: figure not drawn to scale

Basic Geometry

11. A tile factory makes custom tiles, shown above, from two types of stone. If a customer requires 200 tiles, how much black stone will be required?

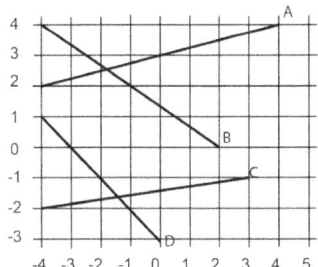

 a. 256 m²
 b. 2560 m²
 c. 2.56 m²
 d. 25.6 m²

12. Which of the lines above represents the equation $2y - x = 4$?

 a. A
 b. B
 c. C
 d. D

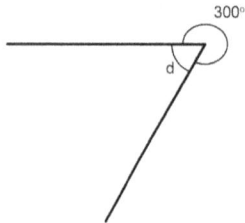

13. What is the measurement of the indicated angle?

    a. 45°
    b. 90°
    c. 60°
    d. 50°

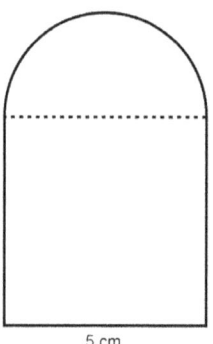

5 cm

Note: figure not drawn to scale

14. What is the perimeter of the above shape?

    a. 22.85 cm
    b. 20 cm
    c. 15 cm
    d. 25.546 cm

Basic Geometry

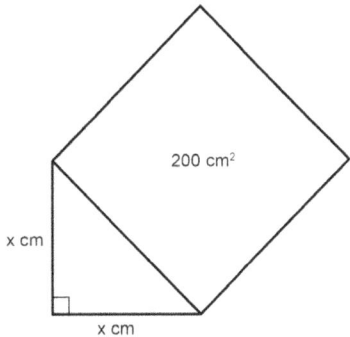

Note: Figure not drawn to scale

15. Assuming the quadrangle in the figure above is square, what is the length of the sides in the triangle above?

    a. 10
    b. 20
    c. 100
    d. 40

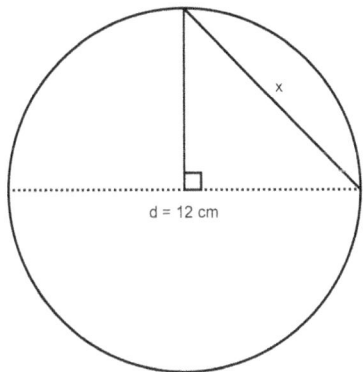

Note: Figure not drawn to scale

16. Calculate the length of side x.

a. 6.46
b. 8.48
c. 3.6
d. 6.4

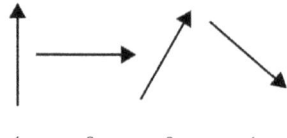

17. What is the correct order of respective slopes for the lines above?

a. Positive, undefined, negative, positive
b. Negative, zero, undefined, positive
c. Undefined, zero, positive, negative
d. Zero, positive undefined, negative

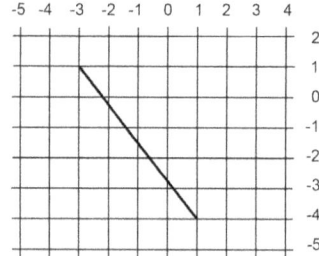

18. What is the slope of the line shown above?

a. 5/4
b. -4/5
c. -5/4
d. -4/5

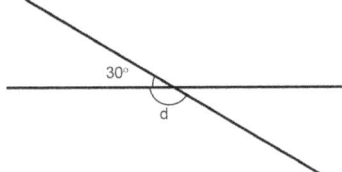

19. What is the indicated angle above?

    a. 150°
    b. 330°
    c. 60°
    d. 120°

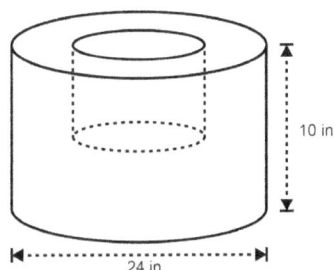

Note: figure not drawn to scale

ACCUPLACER® Math Practice

20. What is the volume of the above solid made by a hollow cylinder that is half the size (in all dimensions) of the larger cylinder?

    a. 1440 π in³

    b. 1260 π in³

    c. 1040 π in³

    d. 960 π in³

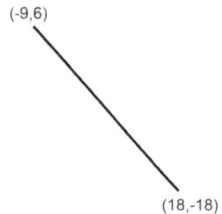

21. What is the slope of the line above?

    a. -8/9

    b. 9/8

    c. -9/8

    d. 8/9

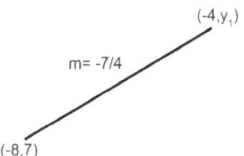

22. With the data given above, what is the value of y_1?

a. 0
b. -7
c. 7
d. 8

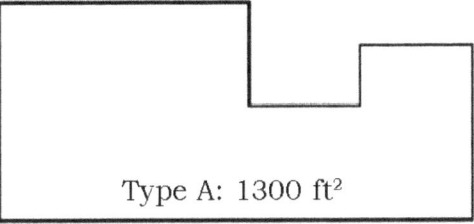

Type A: 1300 ft²

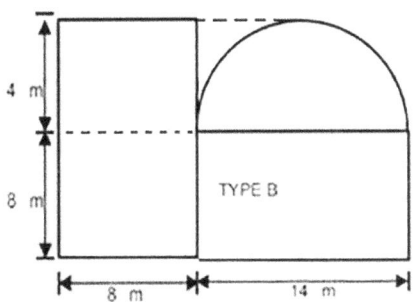

Note: Figure not drawn to scale

ACCUPLACER® Math Practice

23. The price of houses in a certain subdivision is based on the total area. Susan is watching her budget and wants to choose the house with the lowest area. Which house type, A (1300 ft2) or B, should she choose if she would like the house with the lowest price? (1 m² = 10.76 ft² & π = 22/7)

    a. Type B is smaller at 140 ft²
    b. Type A is smaller
    c. Type B is smaller at 855 ft²
    d. Type B is larger

24. How much water can be stored in a cylindrical container 5 meters in diameter and 12 meters high?

Note: figure not drawn to scale

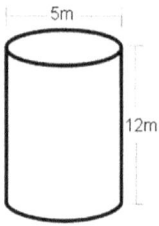

    a. 235.65 m³
    b. 223.65 m³
    c. 240.65 m³
    d. 252.65 m³

Basic Geometry

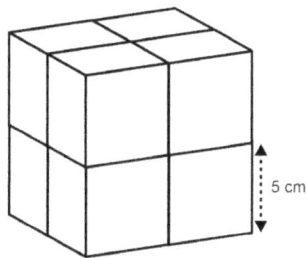

5 cm

Note: figure not drawn to scale

25. Assuming the figure above is composed of cubes, what is the volume?

    a. 125 cm³
    b. 875 cm³
    c. 1000 cm³
    d. 500 cm³

26. Choose the expression the figure represents.

    a. $X > 2$
    b. $X \geq 2$
    c. $X < 2$
    d. $X \leq 2$

ACCUPLACER® Math Practice

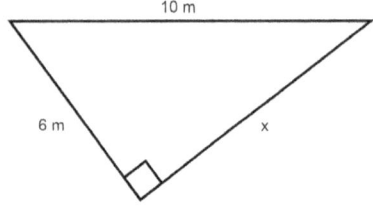

Note: figure not drawn to scale

27. What is the length of the missing side in the triangle above?

    a. 6
    b. 4
    c. 8
    d. 5

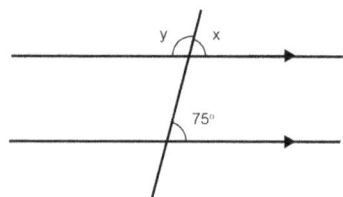

28. What is the value of the angle y?

    a. 25°
    b. 15°
    c. 30°
    d. 105°

29. What is the distance between the two points?

    a. ≈19
    b. 20
    c. ≈21
    d. ≈22

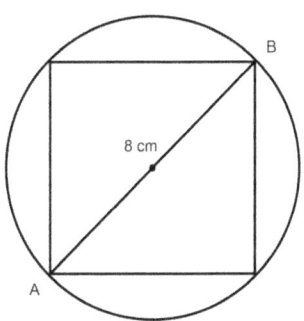

Note: figure not drawn to scale

30. What is area of the circle?

    a. 4 π cm²
    b. 12 π cm²
    c. 10 π cm²
    d. 16 π cm²

ACCUPLACER® Math Practice

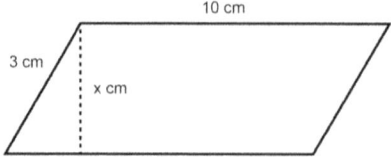

Note: figure not drawn to scale

31. What is the perimeter of the parallelogram above?

a. 12 cm
b. 26 cm
c. 13 cm
d. (13+x) cm

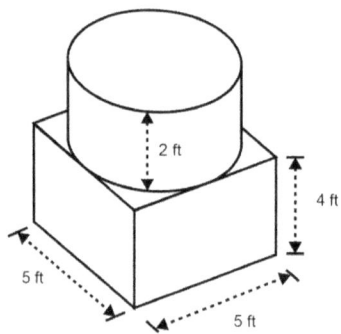

Note: figure not drawn to scale

32. What is the approximate total volume of the above solid?

a. 120 ft³
b. 100 ft³
c. 140 ft³
d. 160 ft³

33. What is the slope of the line above?

    a. 1
    b. 2
    c. 3
    d. -2

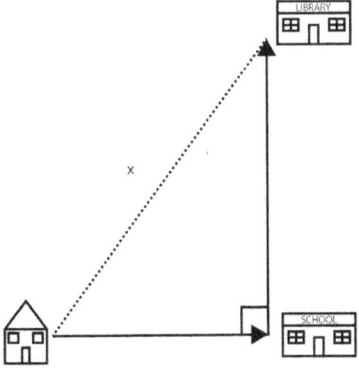

Note: figure not drawn to scale

ACCUPLACER® Math Practice

34. Every day starting from his home Peter travels due east 3 kilometers to the school. After school he travels due north 4 kilometers to the library. What is the distance between Peter's home and the library?

    a. 15 km
    b. 10 km
    c. 5 km
    d. 12 ½ km

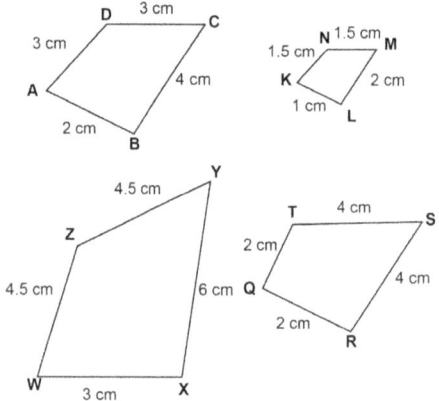

35. Which of the above quadrilaterals are similar?

    a. All are similar
    b. QRST, KLMN, WXYZ
    c. ABCD, KLMN, WXYZ
    d. None of the choices are correct

Basic Geometry

36. Reflect the circle with the center in O with the given mirror line m.

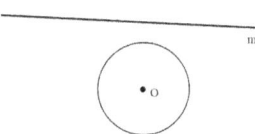

37. Reflect the rectangle ABCD with the given mirror line m in the space below.

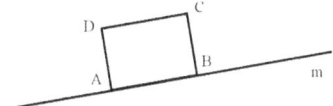

133

ACCUPLACER® Math Practice

38. Reflect the triangle ABC with the given mirror line m in the space below.

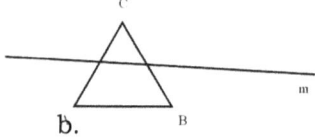

39. Reflect the quadrilateral ABCD in the coordinate plane if the mirror line is y-axis.

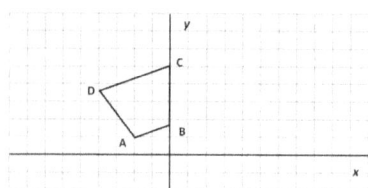

40. Reflect the parallelogram ABCD with the given mirror line m.

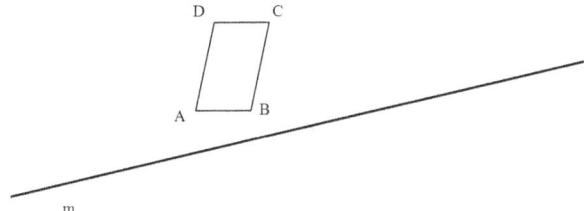

ACCUPLACER® Math Practice

Answer Key

1. A
Point A represents the origin.

2. A
The diagonals of a square intersect at right angles, so each angle measures 90°. Half of that angle will be 45°

3. B
We see that there is a square with side 2 cm and a rectangle adjacent to it, with one side 2 cm (common side with the square) and the other side 4 cm. The perimeter of a shape is found by summing up all sides surrounding the shape, not adding the ones inside the shape. Three 2 cm sides from the square, and two 4 cm sides and one 2 cm side from the rectangle contribute the perimeter.

So, the perimeter of the shape is: 2 + 2 + 2 + 4 + 2 + 4 = 16 cm.

4. C
We are given a large circle and a small circle inside it; with the diameter equal to the radius of the large one. The diameter of the small circle is 4 cm. This means that its radius is 2 cm. Since the diameter of the small circle is the radius of the large circle, the radius of the large circle is 4 cm. The area of a circle is calculated by: πr^2 where r is the radius.

Area of the small circle: $\pi(2)^2 = 4\pi$

Area of the large circle: $\pi(4)^2 = 16\pi$

The difference area is found by:

Area of the large circle - Area of the small circle = $16\pi - 4\pi = 12\pi$

5. B
We see that there are three squares forming a right triangle in the middle. Two of the squares have the areas 81 m² and 144 m². If we denote their sides a and b respectively:

$a^2 = 81$ and $b^2 = 144$. The length, which is asked, is the hypotenuse; a and b are the opposite and adjacent sides of the right angle. By using the Pythagorean Theorem, we can find the value of the asked side:

Pythagorean Theorem:

(Hypotenuse)² = (Opposite Side)² + (Adjacent Side)²

$h^2 = a^2 + b^2$

$a^2 = 81$ and $b^2 = 144$ are given. So;

$h^2 = 81 + 144$

$h^2 = 225$

h = 15 m

6. B
The line is pointing towards numbers less than 1. The equation is therefore, X < 1.

7. D
Comparing respective angles - 70°, 75°, 35°

8. C
Equilateral triangle with 9 cm. sides
Perimeter = 9 + 9 + 9 = 27 cm.

9. D
Perimeter of triangle ABC is asked.
Perimeter of a triangle = sum of all three sides.

Here, Perimeter of △ABC = |AC| + |CB| + |AB|.

Since the triangle is located in the middle of two adjacent and identical rectangles, we find the side lengths using these rectangles:

|AB| = 6 + 6 = 12 cm

|CB| = 8.5 cm

|AC| = |CB| = 8.5 cm

Perimeter = |AC| + |CB| + |AB| = 8.5 + 8.5 + 12 = 29 cm

10. B

https://youtu.be/ZWZ4NoCH7s8?si=vmODb-cBvQVtuXL1

a + b + c + d = ?
The sum of angles around a point is 360°
a + b + c + d = 360°

11. A
Black stone for 200 tiles = 200 x [Total tile area – Inner white area(4 triangles)]

= 200 x [(16^2) - (4 x 1/2 x 8 x 8)]

= 200 x (256 - 128) = 200 x 128 = 25600 cm^2

Converting to meters – 1 cm. = 0.01 meters

= 25600/100 m^2

= 256 m^2

12. A

If a line represents an equation, all points on that line should satisfy the equation. Meaning that all (x, y) pairs present on the line should be able to verify that $2y - x$ is equal to 4. We can find out the correct line by trying a (x, y) point existing on each line. It is easier to choose points on the intersection of the grid lines:

Let us try the point (4, 4) on line A:

2 * 4 - 4 = 4

8 - 4 = 4

4 = 4 ... this is a correct result, so the equation for line A is $2y - x = 4$.

Let us try other points to check the other lines:

Point (-1, 2) on line B:

2 * 2 - (-1) = 4

4 + 1 = 4

5 = 4 ... this is a wrong result, so the equation for line B is not $2y - x = 4$.

Point (3, -1) on line C:

2 * (-1) - 3 = 4

-2 - 3 = 4

-5 = 4 ... this is a wrong result, so the equation for line C is not $2y - x = 4$.

Point (-2, -1) on line D:

2 * (-1) - (-2) = 4

-2 + 2 = 4

0 = 4 ... this is a wrong result, so the equation for line D is not $2y - x = 4$.

13. C
The sum of angles around a point is 360°

d + 300 = 360°

d = 60°

14. A
Find the perimeter of a shape made by merging a square and a semi circle. Perimeter = 3 sides of the square + 1/2 circumference of the circle.
= (3 x 5) + 1/2 (5 π)

= 15 + 2.5 π

= 15 + 7.853975

Perimeter = 22.85 cm

15. A
If we call one side of the square "a," the area of the square will be a^2.

We know that a^2 = 200 cm².

On the other hand; there is an isosceles right triangle. Using the **Pythagorean Theorem:**

(Hypotenuse)² = (Adjacent Side)² + (Opposite Side)²
Where the hypotenuse is equal to one side of the square. So,

$a^2 = x^2 + x^2$

200 = $2x^2$

200/2 = $2x^2$/2

100 = x^2

x = $\sqrt{100}$

x = 10 cm

16. B

In the question, we have a right triangle formed inside the circle. We are asked to find the length of the hypotenuse of this triangle. We can find the other two sides of the triangle by using circle properties:

The diameter of the circle is equal to 12 cm. The legs of the right triangle are the radii of the circle; so they are 6 cm long.

Using the Pythagorean Theorem:

$(Hypotenuse)^2 = (Adjacent\ Side)^2 + (Opposite\ Side)^2$

$x^2 = r^2 + r^2$

$x^2 = 6^2 + 6^2$

$x^2 = 72$

$x = \sqrt{72}$

$x = 8.48$

17. C
Undefined, zero, positive, negative.

18. C
Slope (m) = $\dfrac{\text{change in y}}{\text{change in x}}$

$(x_1, y_1) = (-3, 1)$ & $(x_2, y_2) = (1, -4)$
Slope = $[-4 - 1]/[1-(-3)] = -5/4$

19. A
The angles opposite both angles 30° and angle d are respectively equal to vertical angles.

$2(30° + d) = 360°$

$2d = 360° - 60°$

$2d = 300°$

$d = 150°$

20. B
Total Volume = Volume of large cylinder - Volume of small cylinder

Volume of a cylinder = area of base • height = $\pi r^2 \cdot h$

Total Volume = $(\pi * 12^2 * 10) - (\pi * 6^2 * 5) = 1440\pi - 180\pi$

= 1260π in^3

21. A
If we know the coordinates of two points on a line, we can find the slope (m) with the below formula:

$m = (y_2 - y_1)/(x_2 - x_1)$ where (x_1, y_1) represent the coordinates of one point and (x_2, y_2) the other.

In this question:

$(-9, 6) : x_1 = -9, y_1 = 6$

$(18, -18) : x_2 = 18, y_2 = -18$

Inserting these values into the formula:

$m = (-18 - 6)/(18 - (-9)) = (-24)/(27)$ ... Simplifying by 3:

$m = -8/9$

22. A
If we know the coordinates of two points on a line, we can find the slope (m) with the below formula:
$m = (y_2 - y_1)/(x_2 - x_1)$ where (x_1, y_1) represent the coordinates of one point and (x_2, y_2) the other.

In this question:

$(-4, y_1) : x_1 = -4, y_1 =$ we will find

$(-8, 7) : x_2 = -8, y_2 = 7$

$m = -7/4$

Inserting these values into the formula:

$-7/4 = (7 - y_1)/(-8 - (-4))$

$-7/4 = (7 - y_1)/(-8 + 4)$

$7/(-4) = (7 - y_1)/(-4)$ ... Simplifying the denominators of both sides by -4:

$7 = 7 - y_1$

$0 = -y_1$

$y_1 = 0$

23. D

Area of Type B consists of two rectangles and a half circle. We can find these three areas and sum them up to find the total area:

Area of the left rectangle: $(4 + 8) * 8 = 96 \text{ m}^2$

Area of the right rectangle: $14 * 8 = 112 \text{ m}^2$

The diameter of the circle is equal to 14 m. So, the radius is $14/2 = 7$:

Area of the half circle = $(1/2) * \pi r^2 = (1/2) * (22/7) * (7)^2 = (1 * 22 * 49) / (2 * 7) = 77 \text{ m}^2$

Area of Type B = $96 + 112 + 77 = 285 \text{ m}^2$

Converting this area to ft^2: $285 \text{ m}^2 = 285 \cdot 10.76 \text{ ft}^2 = 3066.6 \text{ ft}^2$

Type B is $(3066.6 - 1300 = 1766.6 \text{ ft}^2)$ 1766.6 ft^2 larger than type A.

24. A

The formula of the volume of cylinder is the base area multiplied by the height. As the formula:

Volume of a cylinder = $\pi r^2 h$. Where π is 3.142, r is radius of the cross sectional area, and h is the height.

We know that the diameter is 5 meters, so the radius is 5/2 = 2.5 meters.

The volume is: V = 3.142 * 2.5² * 12 = 235.65 m³.

25. C
The large cube is made up of 8 smaller cubes with 5 cm sides. The volume of a cube is found by the third power of the length of one side.
Volume of the large cube = Volume of the small cube•8

= (5³) * 8 = 125 * 8

= 1000 cm³

There is another solution for this question. Find the side length of the large cube. There are two cubes rows with 5 cm length for each. So, one side of the large cube is 10 cm.

The volume of this large cube is equal to 10³ = 1000 cm³

26. A
The line is pointing towards numbers greater than 2. The equation is therefore, X > 2.

27. C
Pythagorean Theorem:
(Hypotenuse)² = (Perpendicular)² + (Base)²

h² = a² + b²

Given: a = 6, h = 10

h² = a² + b²

b² = h² - a²

b² = 10² + 6²

b² = 100 – 36

b² = 64

b = 8

28. D
Two parallel lines intersected by a third line with angles of 75°
x = 75° (corresponding angles)
x + y = 180° (supplementary angles)

y = 180° - 75°

y = 105°

29. D
The distance between two points is found by = $[(x_2 - x_1)^2 + (y_2 - y_1)^2]^{1/2}$

In this question:

(18, 12) : $x_1 = 18$, $y_1 = 12$

(9, -6) : $x_2 = 9$, $y_2 = -6$

Distance = $[(9 - 18)^2 + (-6 - 12)^2]^{1/2}$

$= [(-9)^2 + (-18)^2]^{1/2}$

$= (9^2 + 2^2 * 9^2)^{1/2}$

$= (9^2(1 + 4))^{1/2}$ ... We can take 9 out of the square root:

$= 9 * 5^{1/2}$

$= 9\sqrt{5}$

$= 9 * 2.45$

$= 22.05$

The distance is approximately 22 units.

30. D
We have a circle given with diameter 8 cm and a square located within the circle. We are asked to find the area of the circle for which we only need to know the length of the radius that is the half of the diameter.
Area of circle = πr^2 ... r = 8/2 = 4 cm

ACCUPLACER® Math Practice

Area of circle = π * 4²

= 16π cm² ... As we notice, the inner square has no role in this question.

31. B
Perimeter of a parallelogram is the sum of the sides.
Perimeter = 2(l + b)
Perimeter = 2(3 +10), 2 x 13
Perimeter = 26 cm.

32. C
Volume of a cylinder is π x r² x h

Diameter = 5 ft. so radius is 2.5 ft.

Volume of cylinder= π x 2.5² x 2

= π x 6.25 x 2 = 12.5 π

Approximate π to 3.142

Volume of the cylinder = 39.25

Volume of a rectangle = height X width X length.
= 5 X 5 X 4 = 100

Total volume = Volume of rectangular solid + volume of cylinder

Total volume = 100 + 39.25

Total volume = 139.25 ft³ or about 140 ft³

33. B
If we know the coordinates of two points on a line, we can find the slope (m) with the below formula:
m = $(y_2 - y_1)/(x_2 - x_1)$ where (x_1, y_1) represent the coordinates of one point and (x_2, y_2) the other.

In this question:

(-4, -4) : $x_1 = -4$, $y_1 = -4$

$(-1, 2) : x_2 = -1, y_2 = 2$

Inserting these values into the formula:

$m = (2 - (-4))/(-1 - (-4)) = (2 + 4)/(-1 + 4) = 6/3$ ...
Simplifying by 3:

$m = 2$

34. C
Pythagorean Theorem:
$(Hypotenuse)^2 = (Perpendicular)^2 + (Base)^2$

$h^2 = a^2 + b^2$

Given: $3^2 + 4^2 = h^2$

$h^2 = 9 + 16$

$h = \sqrt{25}$

$h = 5$

35. C
Comparing respective sides, ABCD, KLMN, WXYZ are similar.

36.
We reflect the center O against the mirror line m at right angle and we use a compass to draw the circle with the same radius as the original circle.

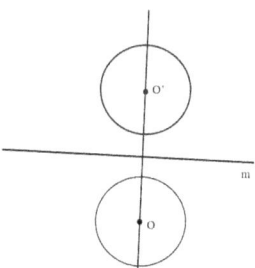

37.

We reflect points C and D against the mirror line m at the right angle. Since points A and B are already on the mirror line, we can't reflect them and that's why A coincides with point A', and the same goes for points B and B'.

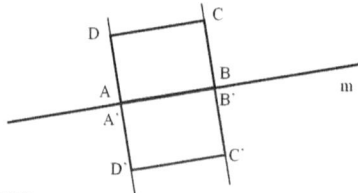

38.

We reflect points A, B and C against the mirror line m at the right angle and we connect the new points A', B' and C'. The process is the same even though the points of the triangle are not on the same side of the mirror line.

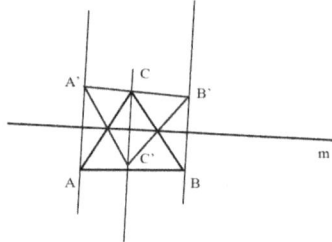

Basic Geometry

39.
The Reflect geometric shapes process is the same in the coordinate plane. Here, our mirror line is y-axis, so we reflect points A and D, and points B and C are already on the mirror line, so we don't reflect them.

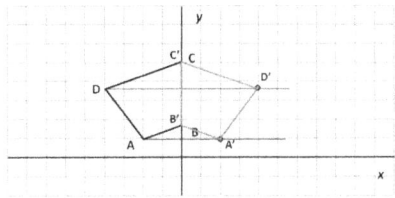

40.
We reflect points A, B, C and D against the mirror line m at right angle and we connect the new points A', B', C' and D'.

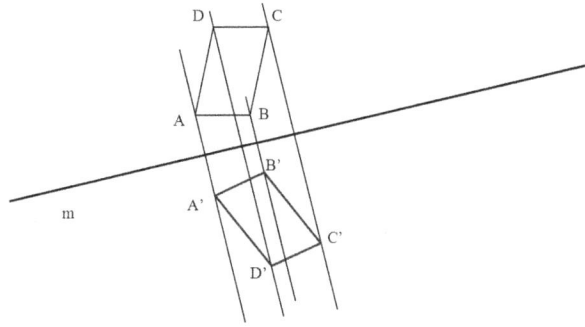

The Power of X: Building Your Algebra Core

Basic Algebra

Basic Algebra

The Basic Algebra section covers the following:

- Ratio and proportion
- Linear equations with 1 and 2 variables
- Quadratics
- Real-world quadratic questions
- Identify quadratic equations from graphs
- Identify linear equations from graphs
- Polynomials
- Solve Geometric problems with Algebra

Solving One-Variable Linear Equations

Linear equations with variable x is an equation with the following form:
$$ax = b$$

where a and b are real numbers. If a=0 and b is different from 0, then the equation has no solution.

Let's solve one simple example of a linear equation with one variable:
$$4x - 2 = 2x + 6$$

When given this type of equation, move variables to one side, and real numbers to the other. Always remember: if you are changing sides, you are changing signs. Move all variables to the left, and real numbers to the right:

4x - 2 = 2x + 6
4x - 2x = 6 + 2
2x = 8
x = 8/2
x = 4

When 2x goes to the left it becomes -2x, and -2 goes to the right and becomes +2. After calculations, we find that x is 4, which is a solution of our linear equation.

Let's solve a little more complex linear equation:

2x - 6/4 + 4 = x
2x - 6 + 16 = 4x
2x - 4x = -16 + 6
-2x = -10
x = -10/-2
x = 5

We multiply whole equation by 4, to lose the fractional line. Now we have a simple linear equation. If we change sides, we change the signs.

Solving Two-Variable Linear Equations

If we have 2 or more linear equations with 2 or more variables, then we have a system of linear equations. The idea here is to express one variable using the other in one equation, and then use it in the second equation, so we get a linear equation with one variable. Here is an example:

$x - y = 3$
$2x + y = 9$

From the first equation, we express y using x.
$y = x - 3$

In the second equation, we write x-3 instead of y. And there we get a linear equation with one variable x.

$2x + x - 3 = 9$
$3x = 9 + 3$
$3x = 12$
$x = 12/3$
$x = 4$

Now that we found x, we can use it to find y.

$y = x - 3$
$y = 4 - 3$
$y = 1$

So, the solution of this system is (x,y) = (4,1).

Let's solve one more system using a different method:

Solve:

$5x - 3y = 17$
$x + 3y = 11$

$5x - 3y + x + 3y = 17 - 11$

Notice that we have -3y in the first equation and +3y in the second. If we add these 2, we get zero, which means we lose variable y. So, we add these 2 equations and we get a linear equation with one variable.

$6x = 6$
$x = 1$
Now that we have x, we use it to find y.

$5 - 3y = 17$
$-3y = 17 - 5$
$-3y = 12$
$y = 12/(-3)$
$y = -4$

Simplifying Polynomials

Let's say we are given some expression with one or more variables, where we have to add, subtract and multiply polynomials. We do the calculations with variables and constants and then we group the variables with the appropriate degrees. As a result, we would get a polynomial. This process is called simplifying polynomials, where we go from a complex expression to a simple polynomial.

ACCUPLACER® Math Practice

Example:

Simplify the following expression and arrange the degrees from bigger to smaller:

$4 + 3x - 2x^2 + 5x + 6x^3 - 2x^2 + 1 = 6x^3 - 4x^2 + 8x + 5$

We can have more complex expressions such as:

$(x + 5)(1 - x) - (2x - 2) = x - x^2 + 5 - 5x - 2x + 2 = -x^2 - 6x + 7$

Here, first we multiply the polynomials and then we subtract the result and the third polynomial.

Factoring Polynomials

If we have a polynomial that we want to write as multiplication of a real number and a polynomial or as a multiplication of 2 or more polynomials, then we are dealing with factoring polynomials.

Let's see an example for a simple factoring:

$12x^2 + 6x - 4 =$
$2 * 6x^2 + 2 * 3x - 2 * 2 =$
$2(6x^2 + 3x - 2)$

We look at every polynomial member as a product of a real number and a variable. Notice that all real numbers in the polynomial are even, so they have the same number (factor). We pull out that 2 in front of the polynomial, and we write what is left.

What if have a more complex case, where we can't find a factor that is a real number? Here is an example:

$x^2 - 2x + 1 =$
$x^2 - x - x + 1 =$
$x(x - 1) - (x - 1) =$
$(x - 1)(x - 1)$

We can write -2x as –x-x . Now we group first 2 members and we see that they have the same factor x, which we can pull in front of them. For the other 2 members, we pull the minus in front of them, so we can get the same binomial that we got with the first 2 members. Now we have that this binomial is the factor for x(x-1) and (x-1).

If we pull x-1 in front (underlined), from the first member we are left with x, and from the second we have -1.
And that is how we transform a polynomial into a product of 2 polynomials (in this case binomials).

Quadratic Equations

A. Factoring

Quadratic equations are usually called second degree equations, which mean that the second degree is the highest degree of the variable that can be found in the quadratic equation. The form of these equations is:

$ax^2 + bx + c = 0$

where a, b and c are some real numbers.

One way for solving quadratic equations is the factoring method, where we transform the quadratic equation into a product of 2 or more polynomials. Let's see how that works in one simple example:

$x^2 + 2x = 0$
$x(x + 2) = 0$
$(x = 0) \lor (x + 2 = 0)$
$(x = 0 \lor (x + -2)$

Notice that here we don't have parameter c, but this is still a quadratic equation, because we have the second degree of variable x. Our factor here is x, which we put in front, and we are left with x+2. The equation is equal to 0, so either x or x+2 are 0, or both are 0.
So, our 2 solutions are 0 and -2.

B. Quadratic formula
If we are unsure how to rewrite quadratic equations so we can solve it using factoring method, we can use the formula for quadratic equation:

$$x_{1,2} = \frac{-b \pm \sqrt{b^2 - 4ac}}{2a}$$

We use $x_{1,2}$ because it represents 2 solutions of the equation. Here is one example:

$3x^2 - 10x + 3 = 0$

$x_{1,2} = \frac{-b \pm \sqrt{b^2 - 4ac}}{2a}$

$x_{1,2} = \frac{-(-10) \pm \sqrt{(-10)^2 - 4 \cdot 3 \cdot 3}}{2 \cdot 3}$

We see that a is 3, b is -10 and c is 3.
We use these numbers in the equation and do some calculations.

$x_{1,2} = \frac{10 \pm \sqrt{100 - 36}}{6}$

$x_{1,2} = \frac{10 \pm \sqrt{64}}{6}$

$x_{1,2} = \frac{10 \pm 8}{6}$

$x_1 = \frac{10+8}{6} = \frac{18}{6} = 3$

$x_2 = \frac{10-8}{6} = \frac{2}{6} = \frac{1}{3}$

Notice that we have + and -, so x_1 is for + and x_2 is for -, and that's how we get 2 solutions.

Quadratic Word Problems

Some real life problems can be solved using quadratic equations. Always try to read carefully so you can write the math problem correctly. Even some geometrical problems can be solved using quadratic equations. Let's solve one real life problem with quadratics:
The distance between 2 cities is 588 kilometers. Train A travels that distance 2 hours and 20 minutes less than train B. How fast are the trains traveling if they differ by 21 km/h?

We first write 2 hours and 20 minutes as a fraction: 20 minutes is one third of the one full hour, so we have:

2 1/3 h = 7/3 h

If we denote with S the distance of 588 km, and V1 is the speed of the train A and V2 is the speed of the train B, and times of the travel are t1 and t2, respectively. Now we can write:

$S = 588$
$V_1 - V_2 = 21 \rightarrow V_2 = V_1 - 21$

$t_1 + 7/3 = t_2$
$V_1 = S/t_1 \rightarrow V_1 t_1 \rightarrow 588 = V_1 t_1 \rightarrow t_1\ 588 / V_1$

$V_2 = S/t_2 \rightarrow S = V_2 t_2 \rightarrow 588 = (V_1 - 21)(t_1 + 7/3)$

$588 = (V_1 - 21)\ (588/V_1 + 7/3)$

$588 = 588 + 7/3\ V_1 - 21 * 588/V_1 - 21\ 7/3$

$0 = 7/x \, V_1 - 3 * 588/v_1 - 7/-3 \, V_1$

$0 = V_1^2 - 5292 - 21 \, V_1$

$V_1^2 - 21 V_1 - 5292 = 0$

$V_{1,2} = (21 \pm \sqrt{441 + 4 * 5292}) / 2$

$V_{1,2} = (21 + 147)/2$

$V_1 = 84$ km/h

$V_2 = 84 - 21 = 63$ km/h

Quadratic Geometry Problems

If length of a hypotenuse of a right triangle is 5, and sum of its legs is 7, find the lengths of its legs.

$a^2 + b^2 = c^2 = 5^2 = 25$

$a + b = 7 \rightarrow a = 7 - b$

$(7 - b)^2 + b^2 = 25$

$49 - 14b + b^2 + b^2 = 25$

$2b^2 - 14b + 24 = 0$

$b^2 - 7b + 24 = 0$

$b_{1,2} = (7 \pm \sqrt{49 - (4 * 12)}) / 2$

$b_{1,2} = 7 \pm \sqrt{(49 - 48)}/2$

$b_{1,2} = (7 \pm 1)/2$

$b_1 = 4$

$b_2 = 3$

$a_1 = 7 - 4 = 3$
$a_2 = 7 - 3 = 4$

Common Algebra Mistakes on Tests

Algebra tests often trip students up not because they don't understand the concepts, but because of small, consistent mechanical errors. Below is a list of the most frequent mistakes, categorized by type, along with how to fix them.

1. The "Invisible" Parentheses (Sign Errors)
This is arguably the #1 cause of lost marks. Students often forget that a negative sign in front of a term applies to the entire term, especially during substitution or distribution.

The Mistake: Writing -3^2 when you mean $(-3)^2$.

Why it matters: -3^2 means "the negative of 3^2" (which is -9), whereas $(-3)^2$ means "negative 3 times negative 3" (which is positive 9).

2. The Distribution Trap: When subtracting a polynomial, students often forget to distribute the negative to the second or third term.

Wrong: $5x - (2x + 3) = 5x - 2x + 3$
Right: $5x - (2x + 3) = 5x - 2x - 3$

2. The "Freshman's Dream" (Exponent Errors)

This nickname describes the very common error of distributing an exponent across addition or subtraction.

The Mistake: Assuming $(x + y)^2 = x^2 + y^2$.

Why it's wrong: Squaring a binomial requires FOIL (First, Outer, Inner, Last). You are missing the middle term.

Right: $(x + y)^2 = (x + y)(x + y) = x^2 + 2xy + y^2$.

Radical Version: Doing the same with square roots, thinking $\sqrt{x^2 + y^2} = x + y$. This is incorrect. (Think of the Pythagorean theorem: $\sqrt{3^2 + 4^2} = \sqrt{25} = 5$, not $3 + 4 = 7$)

3. Illegal Cancellation in Fractions

Students see a matching number on top and bottom and have an urge to "cancel" it, regardless of the operation.

The Mistake: Canceling terms that are bound by addition.

Wrong: $\{x^2 + 5\} / \{x\} \rightarrow x + 5$ (You cannot cancel the x because it is not a factor of the entire numerator).

Right: The expression cannot be simplified simply by canceling. You would have to split it:
$x^2/x + 5/x = x + 5/x$.

Rule of Thumb: You can only cancel factors (things being multiplied), never terms (things being added/subtracted).

4. Order of Operations (PEMDAS/BODMAS)

The Mistake: Adding before multiplying because the addition appears first on the left.

Problem: 6 + 4 X 2.

Wrong: 10 X 2 = 20.
Right: 6 + 8 = 14.

The "Left-to-Right" Blind Spot: For equal-priority operations (Multiplication/Division or Addition/Subtraction), you must go left to right.

Problem: 12 / 4 X 3.
Wrong: 12 / 12 = 1 (Multiplying first).
Right: 3 X 3 = 9 (Dividing first, because it's on the left).

5. Equation Balancing

The Mistake: Performing an operation on one side but not the entire other side.

Scenario: x + 2 = 3x. The student decides to divide by x.
Wrong: 1 + 2 = 3 (Forgot to divide the 2 by x as well).
Right: 1 + 2 / x = 3.

ACCUPLACER® Math Practice

Answer Sheet

	A B C D E		A B C D E
1	○ ○ ○ ○ ○	26	○ ○ ○ ○ ○
2	○ ○ ○ ○ ○	27	○ ○ ○ ○ ○
3	○ ○ ○ ○ ○	28	○ ○ ○ ○ ○
4	○ ○ ○ ○ ○	29	○ ○ ○ ○ ○
5	○ ○ ○ ○ ○	30	○ ○ ○ ○ ○
6	○ ○ ○ ○ ○	31	○ ○ ○ ○ ○
7	○ ○ ○ ○ ○	32	○ ○ ○ ○ ○
8	○ ○ ○ ○ ○	33	○ ○ ○ ○ ○
9	○ ○ ○ ○ ○	34	○ ○ ○ ○ ○
10	○ ○ ○ ○ ○	35	○ ○ ○ ○ ○
11	○ ○ ○ ○ ○	36	○ ○ ○ ○ ○
12	○ ○ ○ ○ ○	37	○ ○ ○ ○ ○
13	○ ○ ○ ○ ○	38	○ ○ ○ ○ ○
14	○ ○ ○ ○ ○	39	○ ○ ○ ○ ○
15	○ ○ ○ ○ ○	40	○ ○ ○ ○ ○
16	○ ○ ○ ○ ○	41	○ ○ ○ ○ ○
17	○ ○ ○ ○ ○	42	○ ○ ○ ○ ○
18	○ ○ ○ ○ ○	43	○ ○ ○ ○ ○
19	○ ○ ○ ○ ○	44	○ ○ ○ ○ ○
20	○ ○ ○ ○ ○	45	○ ○ ○ ○ ○
21	○ ○ ○ ○ ○		
22	○ ○ ○ ○ ○		
23	○ ○ ○ ○ ○		
24	○ ○ ○ ○ ○		
25	○ ○ ○ ○ ○		

Basic Algebra Practice

1. Solve the linear equation: $-x - 7 = -3x - 9$

    a. -1
    b. 0
    c. 1
    d. 2

2. Solve the system: $4x - y = 5 \quad x + 2y = 8$

    a. (3,2)
    b. (3,3)
    c. (2,3)
    d. (2,2)

3. Simplify the following expression:

$3x^3 + 2x^2 + 5x - 7 + 4x^2 - 5x + 2 - 3x^3$

    a. $6x^2 - 9$
    b. $6x^2 - 5$
    c. $6x^2 - 10x - 5$
    d. $6x^2 + 10x - 9$

4. Find 2 numbers that sum to 21 and the sum of the squares is 261.

    a. 14 and 7
    b. 15 and 6
    c. 16 and 5
    d. 17 and 4

ACCUPLACER® Math Practice

5. Using the factoring method, solve the quadratic equation: $x^2 + 4x + 4 = 0$

   a. 0 and 1
   b. 1 and 2
   c. 2
   d. -2

6. Using the quadratic formula, solve the quadratic equation: $x - 31/x = 0$

   a. $-\sqrt{13}$ and $\sqrt{13}$
   b. $-\sqrt{31}$ and $\sqrt{31}$
   c. $-\sqrt{31}$ and $2\sqrt{31}$
   d. $-\sqrt{3}$ and $\sqrt{3}$

7. Using the factoring method, solve the quadratic equation: $2x^2 - 3x = 0$

   a. 0 and 1.5
   b. 1.5 and 2
   c. 2 and 2.5
   d. 0 and 2

8. Using the quadratic formula, solve the quadratic equation: $x^2 - 9x + 14 = 0$

   a. 2 and 7
   b. -2 and 7
   c. -7 and -2
   d. -7 and 2

— Basic Algebra —

9. Solve the following equation $4(y + 6) = 3y + 30$

   a. $y = 20$
   b. $y = 6$
   c. $y = 30/7$
   d. $y = 30$

10. Using the factoring method, solve the quadratic equation: $x^2 - 5x - 6 = 0$

    a. -6 and 1
    b. -1 and 6
    c. 1 and 6
    d. -6 and -1

11. Factor the polynomial $x^3y^3 - x^2y^8$.

    a. $x^2y^3(x - y^5)$
    b. $x^3y^3(1 - y^5)$
    c. $x^2y^2(x - y^6)$
    d. $xy^3(x - y^5)$

12. Find the solution for the following linear equation: $5x/2 = (3x + 24)/6$

    a. -1
    b. 0
    c. 1
    d. 2

ACCUPLACER® Math Practice

13. Solve the system, if a is some real number:

$ax + y = 1$
$x + ay = 1$

    a. (1, a)
    b. (1/a + 1, 1)
    c. (1/(a + 1), 1/(a + 1))
    d. (a, 1/a + 1)

14. Solve $3(x + 2) - 2(1 - x) = 4x + 5$

    a. -1
    b. 0
    c. 1
    d. 2

15. Simplify $3x^a + 6a^x - x^a + (-5a^x) - 2x^a$

    a. $a^x + x^a$
    b. $a^x - x^a$
    c. a^x
    d. x^a

16. A map uses a scale of 1:100,000. How much distance on the ground is 3 inches on the map if the scale is in inches?

    a. 13 inches
    b. 300,000 inches
    c. 30,000 inches
    d. 333.999 inches

17. Using the quadratic formula, solve the quadratic equation: $0.9x^2 + 1.8x - 2.7 = 0$

   a. 1 and 3
   b. -3 and 1
   c. -3 and -1
   d. -1 and 3

18. Find x and y from the following system of equations:

$(4x + 5y)/3 = ((x - 3y)/2) + 4$
$(3x + y)/2 = ((2x + 7y)/3) - 1$

   a. (1, 3)
   b. (2, 1)
   c. (1, 1)
   d. (0, 1)

19. Using the factoring method, solve the quadratic equation: $x^2 + 12x - 13 = 0$

   c. a. -13 and 1
   d. b. -13 and -1
   e. c. 1 and 13
   f. d. -1 and 13

20. Using the quadratic formula, solve the quadratic equation: $((x^2 + 4x + 4) + (x^2 - 4x + 4)) / (x^2 - 4) = 0$.

   a. It has infinite numbers of solutions
   b. 0 and 1
   c. It has no solutions
   d. 0

ACCUPLACER® Math Practice

21. Turn the following expression into a simple polynomial: $5(3x^2 - 2) - x^2(2 - 3x)$

    a. $3x^3 + 17x^2 - 10$

    b. $3x^3 + 13x^2 + 10$

    c. $-3x^3 - 13x^2 - 10$

    d. $3x^3 + 13x^2 - 10$

22. Solve $(x^3 + 2)(x^2 - x) - x^5$.

    a. $2x^5 - x^4 + 2x^2 - 2x$

    b. $-x^4 + 2x^2 - 2x$

    c. $-x^4 - 2x^2 - 2x$

    d. $-x^4 + 2x^2 + 2x$

23. $9ab^2 + 8ab^2 =$

    a. ab^2

    b. $17ab^2$

    c. 17

    d. $17a^2b^2$

24. Factor the polynomial $x^2 - 7x - 30$.

    a. $(x + 15)(x - 2)$

    b. $(x + 10)(x - 3)$

    c. $(x - 10)(x + 3)$

    d. $(x - 15)(x + 2)$

Basic Algebra

25. If a and b are real numbers, solve the following equation: $(a + 2)x - b = -2 + (a + b)x$

    a. -1
    b. 0
    c. 1
    d. 2

26. Turn the following expression into a simple polynomial: $1 - x(1 - x(1 - x))$

    a. $x^3 + x^2 - x + 1$
    b. $-x^3 - x^2 + x + 1$
    c. $-x^3 + x^2 - x + 1$
    d. $x^3 + x^2 - x - 1$

27. $7(2y + 8) + 1 - 4(y + 5) =$

    a. $10y + 36$
    b. $10y + 77$
    c. $18y + 37$
    d. $10y + 37$

28. Richard gives 's' amount of salary to each of his 'n' employees weekly. If he has 'x' amount of money then how many days he can employ these 'n' employees.

    a. sx/7
    b. 7x/nx
    c. nx/7s
    d. 7x/ns

ACCUPLACER® Math Practice

29. Factor the polynomial $x^2 - 3x - 4$.

    a. $(x + 1)(x - 4)$
    b. $(x - 1)(x + 4)$
    c. $(x - 1)(x - 4)$
    d. $(x + 1)(x + 4)$

30. Using the quadratic formula, solve the quadratic equation:

$(a^2 - b^2)x^2 + 2ax + 1 = 0$

    a. $a/(a + b)$ and $b/(a + b)$
    b. $1/(a + b)$ and $a/(a + b)$
    c. $a/(a + b)$ and $a/(a - b)$
    d. $-1/(a + b)$ and $-1/(a - b)$

31. Turn the following expression into a simple polynomial: $(a + b)(x + y) + (a - b)(x - y) - (ax + by)$

    a. $ax + by$
    b. $ax - by$
    c. $ax^2 + by^2$
    d. $ax^2 - by^2$

32. The area of a rectangle is 20 cm². If one side increases by 1 cm and other by 2 cm, the area of the new rectangle is 35 cm². Find the sides of the original rectangle.

    a. (4,8)
    b. (4,5)
    c. (2.5,8)
    d. b and c

33. Find the x-intercepts of the quadratic function f(x) = (x - 5)² - 9.

   a. {2,4}
   b. {2,8}
   c. {4,8}
   d. {1,2}

34. In a store, the price of t-shirts and pants are constant. If John buys 4 t-shirts and 5 pair of pants, he pays $51. If he buys 7 t-shirts and 3 pair of pants, then he pays $49. Find the difference between the price of one pair of pants and one t-shirt.

   a. 0
   b. 3
   c. 7
   d. 12

35. Which of the following graphs represent the equation 4x - y = 6?

a.

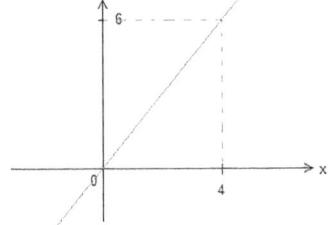

b.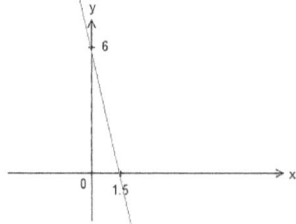

c.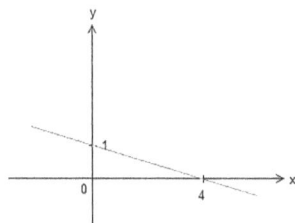

d.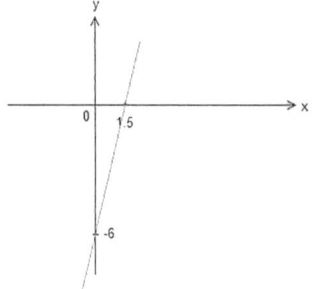

36. A number is increased by 2 and then multiplied by 3. The result is 24. What is this number?

    a. 4
    b. 6
    c. 8
    d. 10

Basic Algebra

37. My father's age divided by 5 is equal to my brother's age divided by 3. My brother is 3 years older than me. My father's age is 3 less than 2 times my age. How old is my father?

    a. 34
    b. 45
    c. 56
    d. 61

38. $(x - 2) / 4 - (3x + 5) / 7 = -3$, $x = ?$

    a. 6
    b. 7
    c. 10
    d. 13

39. The inner angles of a triangle are given as $x + 20$, $3x - 10$ and $8x + 50$. Find the difference between the smallest and the largest angles.

    a. 65
    b. 75
    c. 110
    d. 150

40. The width of a rectangle is two thirds of the length. The perimeter of this rectangle is 150 cm. Find the length of this shape.

    a. 30 cm
    b. 45 cm
    c. 60 cm
    d. 75 cm

ACCUPLACER® Math Practice

41. The volume of a sphere with radius r is equal to the volume of a cylinder with radius 3r and height h. What is r/h equal to?

    a. 9/4

    b. 9/2

    c. 5

    d. 27/4

42. The area of a triangle is equal to 32 cm² and the height of this triangle is 4 cm less than 3 times the base. What is the length of the height?

    a. 12

    b. 16

    c. 18

    d. 24

43. What is the sum of possible integers for x satisfying $|5x - 3| \leq 7$?

    a. 1

    b. 2

    c. 3

    d. 5

44. What is the multiplication of possible x values satisfying $|7 - 2x| = 9$?

    a. -8

    a. -1

    a. 4

    a. 16

45. Find the solution set for |x − 5| + 8 < 4.

    a. { }
    b. {-3, 4}
    c. {1, 3}
    d. {1, 4}

ACCUPLACER® Math Practice

Answer Key

1. A

We should collect similar terms on the same side. Here, we can collect x terms on left side, and the constants on the right side:

- x - 7 = - 3x - 9 .... Let us add 3x to both sides:

- x - 7 + 3x = - 3x - 9 + 3x

2x - 7 = - 9 ... Now, we can add + 7 to both sides:

2x - 7 + 7 = - 9 + 7

2x = - 2 ... Dividing both sides by 2 gives us the value of x:

x = -2/2

x = -1

2. C

First, we need to write two equations separately:
4x - y = 5 (I)

x + 2y = 8 (II) ... Here, we can use two ways to solve the system. One is substitution method, the other one is linear elimination method:

1. Substitution Method

Equation (I) gives us that y = 4x - 5. We insert this value of y into equation (II):

x + 2(4x - 5) = 8

x + 8x - 10 = 8

9x - 10 = 8

$9x = 18$

$x = 2$

Bu knowing x = 2, we can find the value of y by inserting x = 2 into either of the equations. Let us choose equation (I):

$4(2) - y = 5$

$8 - y = 5$

$8 - 5 = y$

$y = 3 \rightarrow$ solution is (2, 3)

2. Linear Elimination Method:

2•/ 4x - y = 5 ... by multiplying equation (I) by 2, we see that -2y will form; and y terms

   x + 2y = 8 ... will be eliminated when summed with +2y in equation (II):

2•/ 4x - y = 5

+   x + 2y = 8
_____

   8x - 2y = 10

 + x + 2y = 8 ... Summing side by side:

$8x + x - 2y + 2y = 10 + 8$ ... -2y and +2y eliminate each other:

$9x = 18$

$x = 2$

By knowing x = 2, we can find the value of y by inserting x = 2 into either of the equations. Let us choose equation (I):

$4(2) - y = 5$

$8 - y = 5$

$8 - 5 = y$

$y = 3 \rightarrow$ solution is (2, 3)

3. B

$3x^3 + 2x^2 + 5x - 7 + 4x^2 - 5x + 2 - 3x^3$ ... write similar terms together:

$= 3x^3 - 3x^3 + 2x^2 + 4x^2 + 5x - 5x - 7 + 2$ ... operate within the same terms. $3x^3$ and $-3x^3$, $5x$ and $-5x$ cancel:

$= 6x^2 - 5$

4. B

There are two statements made. This means that we can write two equations according to these statements:

The sum of two numbers are 21: $x + y = 21$

The sum of the squares is 261: $x^2 + y^2 = 261$

We are asked to find x and y.

Since we have the sums of the numbers and the sums of their squares; we can use the square formula of $x + y$, that is:

$(x + y)^2 = x^2 + 2xy + y^2$ ... Here, we can insert the known values $x + y$ and $x^2 + y^2$:

$(21)^2 = 261 + 2xy$ ... Arranging to find xy:

$441 = 261 + 2xy$

$441 - 261 = 2xy$

$180 = 2xy$

$xy = 180/2$

— Basic Algebra —

xy = 90

We need to find two numbers which multiply to 90. Checking the answer choices, we see that in (b), 15 and 6 are given. 15•6 = 90. Also their squares sum up to 261 ($15^2 + 6^2 = 225 + 36 = 261$). So these two numbers satisfy the equation.

5. D

$x^2 + 4x + 4 = 0$ ... We try to separate the middle term 4x to find common factors with x^2 and 4 separately:

$x^2 + 2x + 2x + 4 = 0$ ... Here, we see that x is a common factor for x^2 and 2x, and 2 is a common factor for 2x and 4:

x(x + 2) + 2(x + 2) = 0 ... Here, we have x times x + 2 and 2 times x + 2 summed up. This means that we have x + 2 times x + 2:

(x + 2)(x + 2) = 0

$(x + 2)^2 = 0$ ... This is true if only if x + 2 is equal to zero.

x + 2 = 0

x = -2

6. B

To solve the equation, first we need to arrange it to appear in the form $ax^2 + bx + c = 0$ by removing the denominator:

x - 31/x = 0 ... First, we enlarge the equation by x:

x•x - 31•x/x = 0

$x^2 - 31 = 0$

The quadratic formula to find the roots of a quadratic equation is:

$x_{1,2} = (-b \pm \sqrt{\Delta}) / 2a$ where $\Delta = b^2 - 4ac$ and is called the discriminant of the quadratic equation.

In our question, the equation is $x^2 - 31 = 0$. By remembering the form $ax^2 + bx + c = 0$:

$a = 1, b = 0, c = -31$

So, we can find the discriminant first, and then the roots of the equation:

$\Delta = b^2 - 4ac = 0^2 - 4 \cdot 1 \cdot (-31) = 124$

$x_{1,2} = (-b \pm \sqrt{\Delta}) / 2a = (\pm\sqrt{124}) / 2 = (\pm\sqrt{4 \cdot 31}) / 2 = (\pm 2\sqrt{31}) / 2$ ... Simplifying by 2:

$x_{1,2} = \pm\sqrt{31}$ ... This means that the roots are $\sqrt{31}$ and $-\sqrt{31}$.

7. A
$2x^2 - 3x = 0$ ... we see that both of the terms contain x; so we can take it out as a factor:

$x(2x - 3) = 0$ ... two terms are multiplied and the result is zero. This means that either of the terms or, both can be equal to zero:

$x = 0$ ... this is one solution

$2x - 3 = 0 \rightarrow 2x = 3 \rightarrow x = 3/2 \rightarrow x = 1.5$ ... this is the second solution.

So, the solutions are 0 and 1.5.

8. A
To solve the equation, we need the equation in the form $ax^2 + bx + c = 0$.

$x^2 - 9x + 14 = 0$ is already in this form.

The quadratic formula to find the roots of a quadratic

equation is:

$x_{1,2} = (-b \pm \sqrt{\Delta}) / 2a$ where $\Delta = b^2 - 4ac$ and is called the discriminant of the quadratic equation.

In our question, the equation is $x^2 - 9x + 14 = 0$. By remembering the form $ax^2 + bx + c = 0$:

$a = 1, b = -9, c = 14$

So, we can find the discriminant first, and then the roots of the equation:

$\Delta = b^2 - 4ac = (-9)^2 - 4 \times 1 \times 14 = 81 - 56 = 25$

$x_{1,2} = (-b \pm \sqrt{\Delta}) / 2a = (-(-9) \pm \sqrt{25}) / 2 = (9 \pm 5) / 2$

This means that the roots are,

$x_1 = (9 - 5) / 2 = 2$ and $x_2 = (9 + 5) / 2 = 7$

9. B
$4y + 24 = 3y + 30$, $= 4y - 3y + 24 = 30$, $= y + 24 = 30$, $= y = 30 - 24$, $= y = 6$

10. B
$x^2 - 5x - 6 = 0$

We try to separate the middle term $-5x$ to find common factors with x^2 and -6 separately:

$x^2 - 6x + x - 6 = 0$ ... Here, we see that x is a common factor for x^2 and $-6x$:

$x(x - 6) + x - 6 = 0$ ... Here, we have x times $x - 6$ and 1 time $x - 6$ summed up. This means that we have $x + 1$ times $x - 6$:

$(x + 1)(x - 6) = 0$ ... This is true when either or both of the expressions in the parenthesis are equal to zero:

$x + 1 = 0 \ldots x = -1$

x - 6 = 0 ... x = 6

-1 and 6 are the solutions for this quadratic equation.

11. A

We need to find the greatest common divisor of the two terms to factor the expression. We should remember that if the bases of exponent numbers are the same, the multiplication of two terms is found by summing the powers and writing on the same base. Similarly; when dividing, the power of the divisor is subtracted from the power of the divided.

Both x^3y^3 and x^2y^8 contain x^2 and y^3. So;

$x^3y^3 - x^2y^8 = x \cdot x^2y^3 - y^5 \cdot x^2y^3$ ... We can carry x^2y^3 out as the factor:

$= x^2y^3(x - y^5)$

12. D

Our aim to collect the knowns on one side and the unknowns (x terms) on the other side:

$5x/2 = (3x + 24)/6$ ... First, we can simplify the denominators of both sides by 2:

$5x = (3x + 24)/3$ ... Now, we can cross multiply:

$15x = 3x + 24$

$15x - 3x = 24$

$12x = 24$

$x = 24/12 = 2$

Basic Algebra

13. C
Solving the system means finding x and y. Since we also have a in the system, we will find x and y depending on a.

We can obtain y by using the equation $ax + y = 1$:

$y = 1 - ax$ ... Then, we can insert this value into the second equation:

$x + a(1 - ax) = 1$

$x + a - a^2x = 1$

$x - a^2x = 1 - a$

$x(1 - a^2) = 1 - a$ ... We need to obtain x alone:

$x = (1 - a)/(1 - a^2)$ ... Here, $1 - a^2 = (1 - a)(1 + a)$ is used:

$x = (1 - a)/((1 - a)(1 + a))$ ... Simplifying by $(1 - a)$:

$x = 1/(a + 1)$ ... Now we know the value of x. By using either of the equations, we can find the value of y. Let us use $y = 1 - ax$:

$y = 1 - a \cdot 1/(a + 1)$

$y = 1 - a/(a + 1)$ ... By writing on the same denominator:

$y = ((a + 1) - a)/(a + 1)$

$y = (a + 1 - a)/(a + 1)$ ... a and -a cancel each other:

$y = 1/(a + 1)$ ... x and y are found to be equal.

The solution of the system is $(1/(a + 1), 1/(a + 1))$

14. C
To solve the linear equation, we operate the knowns and unknowns within each other and try to obtain x term (which is the unknown) alone on one side of the equation:
$3(x + 2) - 2(1 - x) = 4x + 5$ ... We remove the parenthesis

by distributing the factors:

3x + 6 - 2 + 2x = 4x + 5

5x + 4 = 4x + 5

5x - 4x = 5 - 4

x = 1

15. C
Here, we use the commutative property of multiplication, meaning that xa = ax:
3xa + 6ax - xa + (-5ax) - 2xa = 3ax + 6ax - ax - 5ax - 2ax
= (3 + 6 - 1 - 5 - 2)ax
= (9 - 8)ax
= ax

16. B
1 inch on map = 100,000 inches on ground. So 3 inches on map = 3 x 100,000 = 300,000 inches on ground.

17. B
To solve the equation, we need the equation in the form ax2 + bx + c = 0.

$0.9x^2$ + 1.8x - 2.7 = 0 is already in this form.

The quadratic formula to find the roots of a quadratic equation is:

$x_{1,2}$ = (-b ± √Δ) / 2a where Δ = b^2 - 4ac and is called the discriminant of the quadratic equation.

In our question, the equation is $0.9x^2$ + 1.8x - 2.7 = 0. To eliminate the decimals, let us multiply the equation by 10: $9x^2$ + 18x - 27 = 0 ... This equation can be simplified by 9 since each term contains 9:

x^2 + 2x - 3 = 0

— Basic Algebra —

By remembering the form $ax^2 + bx + c = 0$:

$a = 1, b = 2, c = -3$

So, we can find the discriminant first, and then the roots of the equation:

$\Delta = b^2 - 4ac = (2)^2 - 4 \cdot 1 \cdot (-3) = 4 + 12 = 16$

$x_{1,2} = (-b \pm \sqrt{\Delta}) / 2a = (-2 \pm \sqrt{16}) / 2 = (-2 \pm 4) / 2$

This means that the roots are,

$x_1 = (-2 - 4)/2 = -3$ and $x_2 = (-2 + 4)/2 = 1$

18. C
First, we need to arrange the two equations to obtain the form $ax + by = c$. We see that there are 3 and 2 in the denominators of both equations. If we equate all at 6, then we can cancel all 6 in the denominators and have straight equations:

Equate all denominators at 6:

$2(4x + 5y)/6 = 3(x - 3y)/6 + 4 \cdot 6/6$ ... Now we can cancel 6 in the denominators:

$8x + 10y = 3x - 9y + 24$ ... We can collect x and y terms on left side of the equation:

$8x + 10y - 3x + 9y = 24$

$5x + 19y = 24$ ... Equation (I)
Arrange the second equation:

$3(3x + y)/6 = 2(2x + 7y)/6 - 1 * 6/6$ ... Now we can cancel 6 in the denominators:

$9x + 3y = 4x + 14y - 6$ ... We can collect x and y terms on left side of the equation:

$9x + 3y - 4x - 14y = -6$

$5x - 11y = -6$ ... Equation (II)

Now, we have two equations and two unknowns x and y. By writing the two equations one under the other and operating, we can find one unknown first, and find the other next:

$5x + 19y = 24$
$-1/ 5x - 11y = -6$ ... If we substitute this equation from the upper one, 5x cancels -5x:

$5x + 19y = 24$

$-5x + 11y = 6$ ... Summing side-by-side:

$5x - 5x + 19y + 11y = 24 + 6$

$30y = 30$ ... Dividing both sides by 30:
$y = 1$

Inserting y = 1 into either of the equations, we can find the value of x. Choosing equation I:

$5x + 19 \cdot 1 = 24$

$5x = 24 - 19$

$5x = 5$ ... Dividing both sides by 5:

$x = 1$

So, x = 1 and y = 1 is the solution; shown as (1, 1).

19. A
$x^2 + 12x - 13 = 0$ ... We try to separate the middle term 12x to find common factors with x^2 and -13 separately:

Basic Algebra

$x^2 + 13x - x - 13 = 0$ ... Here, we see that x is a common factor for x^2 and 13x, and -1 is a common factor for -x and -13:

$x(x + 13) - 1(x + 13) = 0$ ... Here, we have x times x + 13 and -1 times x + 13 summed up. This means that we have x - 1 times x + 13:

$(x - 1)(x + 13) = 0$

This is true when either, or both, the expressions in the parenthesis are equal to zero:

x - 1 = 0 ... x = 1

x + 13 = 0 ... x = -13

1 and -13 are the solutions for this quadratic equation.

20. C
First, we need to simplify the equation:
$((x^2 + 4x + 4) + (x^2 - 4x + 4)) / (x^2 - 4) = 0$

$(x^2 + 4x + 4 + x^2 - 4x + 4) / (x^2 - 4) = 0$ ... 4x and -4x in the numerator cancel.

Note that $x^2 - 4$ is two square difference and is equal to $x^2 - 2^2 = (x - 2)(x + 2)$:

$(2x^2 + 8)/((x - 2)(x + 2)) = 0$

The denominator tells us that if x - 2 or x + 2 equals to zero, there will be no solution. So, we will need to eliminate x = 2 and x = -2 from our solution which will be found considering the numerator:

$2x^2 + 8 = 0$

$2(x^2 + 4) = 0$

$x^2 + 4 = 0$

$x^2 = -4$ ... We know that, a square cannot be equal to a negative number. Solution for the square root of -4 is not a real number, so this equation has no solution.

21. D
We need to distribute the factors to the terms inside the related parenthesis:

$5(3x^2 - 2) - x^2(2 - 3x) = 15x^2 - 10 - (2x^2 - 3x^3)$

$= 15x^2 - 10 - 2x^2 + 3x^3$

$= 3x^3 + 15x^2 - 2x^2 - 10$ ... similar terms written together to ease summing/substituting.

$= 3x^3 + 13x^2 - 10$

22. B
We need to distribute the factors to the terms inside the related parenthesis:

$(x^3 + 2)(x^2 - x) - x^5 = x^5 - x^4 + (2x^2 - 2x) - x^5$

$= x^5 - x^4 + 2x^2 - 2x - x^5$

$= x^5 - x^5 - x^4 + 2x^2 - 2x$ ... similar terms written together to ease summing/substituting.

$= -x^4 + 2x^2 - 2x$

23. B
To simplify the expression, we need to find common factors. We see that both terms contain the term ab^2. So, we can take this term out of each term as a factor:

$9ab^2 + 8ab^2 = (9 + 8)ab^2 = 17ab^2$

Basic Algebra

24. C
$x^2 - 7x - 30 = 0$ ... We try to separate the middle term $-7x$ to find common factors with x^2 and -30 separately:

$x^2 - 10x + 3x - 30 = 0$ ... Here, we see that x is a common factor for x^2 and $-10x$, and 3 is a common factor for $3x$ and -30:

$x(x - 10) + 3(x - 10) = 0$ ... Here, we have x times $x - 10$ and 3 times $x - 10$ summed up. This means that we have $x + 3$ times $x - 10$:
$(x + 3)(x - 10) = 0$ or $(x - 10)(x + 3) = 0$

25. A
We need to simplify the equation by distributing factors and then collecting x terms on one side, and the others on the other side:

$(a + 2)x - b = -2 + (a + b)x$

$ax + 2x - b = -2 + ax + bx$

$ax + 2x - ax - bx = -2 + b$ ... ax and -ax cancel each other:

$2x - bx = -2 + b$ ... we take -1 as a factor on the right side:

$(2 - b)x = -(2 - b)$

$x = -(2 - b)/(2 - b)$ ... Simplifying by $2 - b$:

$x = -1$

26. C
To obtain a polynomial, remove the parenthesis by distributing the related factors to the terms inside the parenthesis:
$1 - x(1 - x(1 - x)) = 1 - x(1 - (x - x * x)) = 1 - x(1 - x + x^2)$

$= 1 - (x - x * x + x * x^2) = 1 - x + x^2 - x^3$ ... Writing this result in descending order of powers:

$= -x^3 + x^2 - x + 1$

27. D

To simplify the expression, remove the parenthesis by distributing the related factors to the terms inside the parenthesis:

$7(2y + 8) + 1 - 4(y + 5)$
$= (7 * 2y + 7 * 8) + 1 - (4 * y + 4 * 5)$

$= 14y + 56 + 1 - 4y - 20$

$= 14y - 4y + 56 + 1 - 20$ ... similar terms written together to ease summing/substituting.

$= 10y + 37$

28. D

We are given that each of the n employees earns s amount of salary weekly. This means that one employee earns s salary weekly. So; Richard has 'ns' amount of money to employ n employees for a week.

We are asked to find the number of days n employees can be employed with x amount of money. We can do simple direct proportion:

If Richard can employ 'n' employees for 7 days with 'ns' amount of money,

Richard can employ n employees for y days with x amount of money ... y is the number of days we need to find.

Cross multiply:

$y = (x * 7)/(ns)$

$y = 7x/ns$

― Basic Algebra ―

29. A

$x^2 - 3x - 4$ ... try to separate the middle term $-3x$ to find common factors with x^2 and -4 separately:

$x^2 + x - 4x - 4$ ... Here, x is a common factor for x^2 and x, and -4 is a common factor for $-4x$ and -4:

$= x(x + 1) - 4(x + 1)$ ... Here, x times $x + 1$ and -4 times $x + 1$ summed up. This means that we have $x - 4$ times $x + 1$:

$= (x - 4)(x + 1)$ or $(x + 1)(x - 4)$

30. D

To solve the equation, we need the equation in the form $ax^2 + bx + c = 0$.

$(a^2 - b^2)x^2 + 2ax + 1 = 0$ is already in this form.

The quadratic formula to find the roots of a quadratic equation is:

$x_{1,2} = (-b \pm \sqrt{\Delta}) / 2a$ where $\Delta = b^2 - 4ac$ and is called the discriminant of the quadratic equation.

In our question, the equation is $(a^2 - b^2)x^2 + 2ax + 1 = 0$.

By remembering the form $ax^2 + bx + c = 0$: $a = a^2 - b^2$, $b = 2a$, $c = 1$

So, we can find the discriminant first, and then the roots of the equation:

$\Delta = b^2 - 4ac = (2a)^2 - 4(a^2 - b^2) * 1 = 4a^2 - 4a^2 + 4b^2 = 4b^2$

$x_{1,2} = (-b \pm \sqrt{\Delta}) / 2a = (-2a \pm \sqrt{4b^2}) / (2(a^2 - b^2)) = (-2a \pm 2b) / (2(a^2 - b^2))$

$= 2(-a \pm b) / (2(a^2 - b^2))$ ... We can simplify by 2:

$= (-a \pm b) / (a^2 - b^2)$

This means that the roots are,

$x_1 = (-a - b) / (a^2 - b^2)$ ... $a^2 - b^2$ is two square differences:

$x_1 = -(a + b) / ((a - b)(a + b))$ ... $(a + b)$ terms cancel:

$x_1 = -1/(a - b)$

$x_2 = (-a + b) / (a^2 - b^2)$ ... $a^2 - b^2$ is two square differences:

$x_2 = -(a - b) / ((a - b)(a + b))$ ... $(a - b)$ terms cancel:

$x_2 = -1/(a + b)$

31. A
To simplify, remove the parenthesis and see if any terms cancel:

$(a + b)(x + y) + (a - b)(x - y) - (ax + by) = ax + ay + bx + by + ax - ay - bx + by - ax - by$

Writing similar terms together:

$= ax + ax - ax + bx - bx + ay - ay + by + by - by$ ... + terms cancel - terms:

$= ax + by$

32. D
The area of a rectangle is found by multiplying the width to the length. If we call these sides with "a" and "b"; the area is $= a * b$.

We are given that $a * b = 20$ cm² ... Equation I

One side is increased by 1 and the other by 2 cm. So new side lengths are "a + 1" and "b + 2."

The new area is $(a + 1)(b + 2) = 35$ cm² ... Equation II

Using equations I and II, we can find a and b:

$ab = 20$

$(a + 1)(b + 2) = 35$ ... distribute the terms in parenthesis:

$ab + 2a + b + 2 = 35$

Insert $ab = 20$ to the above equation:

$20 + 2a + b + 2 = 35$

$2a + b = 35 - 2 - 20$

$2a + b = 13$ ... This is one equation with two unknowns. We need to use another information to have two equations with two unknowns which leads us to the solution. We know that $ab = 20$. So, we can use $a = 20/b$:

$2(20/b) + b = 13$

$40/b + b = 13$ ... equate all denominators to "b" and eliminate it:

$40 + b^2 = 13b$

$b^2 - 13b + 40 = 0$ ... use the roots by factoring. We try to separate the middle term $-13b$ to find common factors with b^2 and 40 separately:

$b^2 - 8b - 5b + 40 = 0$ ... Here, b is a common factor for b^2 and $-8b$, and -5 is a common factor for $-5b$ and 40:

$b(b - 8) - 5(b - 8) = 0$ Here, b times $b - 8$ and -5 times $b - 8$ summed up. This means that we have $b - 5$ times $b - 8$:

$(b - 5)(b - 8) = 0$

This is true when either or both of the expressions in the parenthesis are equal to zero:

$b - 5 = 0$ ... $b = 5$

$b - 8 = 0$ ... $b = 8$

So we have two values for b which means we have two

values for a as well. To find a, we can use any equation we have. Let us use a = 20/b.

If b = 5, a = 20/b → a = 4

If b = 8, a = 20/b → a = 2.5

So, (a, b) pairs for the sides of the original rectangle are: (4, 5) and (2.5, 8). These are found in (b) and (c) answer choices.

33. B
Finding the x-intercepts of a function means that we need to equate the function to zero and find the roots of the equation:

$(x - 5)^2 - 9 = 9$

$(x - 5)^2 = 9$

$\sqrt{(x - 5)^2} = \sqrt{9}$

x - 5 = 3 → x = 8

x - 5 = -3 → x = 2

34. B
We have two variables: the price of a t-shirt and a pair of pants; and we have two situations given about them. We need to set two equations and solve them for the variables. Then, we are asked to find the difference.

Let us call the price of a t-shirt by a, and the price of a pair of pants by b:

If John buys 4 t-shirts and 5 pair of pants, he pays $51 → 4a + 5b = 51

If he buys 7 t-shirts and 3 pair of pants, then he pays $49 → 7a + 3b = 49

4a + 5b = 51

7a + 3b = 49

We have two paths to follow: substitution or elimination. Here, since extracting a or b from either equation results in fractions; it is easier to choose elimination:

-3/ 4a + 5b = 51

5/ 7a + 3b = 49

-12a - 15b = -153

<u>35a + 15b = 245</u>

      23a = 92

        a = 4

Choosing either of the equations, find b, by inserting a:

4 * 4 + 5b = 51

16 + 5b = 51

5b = 35

b = 7

The difference between a and b is 7 - 4 = 3.

35. D
The simplest way to draw the graph of a linear equation is to insert zero into x and y separately and to obtain two points on the line.

4x - y = 6 is the equation of the line.

If x = 0, y = - 6 → point (0, - 6) is obtained

If y = 0, x = 6/4 = 1.5 → point (1.5, 0) is obtained

Line 4x - y = 6 passes through (0, - 6) and (1.5, 0)

The graph satisfying the condition is given in choice D.

36. B
Let us call this number by x:

This number is increased by 2: x + 2

Then, it is multiplied by 3: 3(x + 2)

The result is 24: 3(x + 2) = 24 ... Solving this linear equation, we obtain the value of the number:

x + 2 = 24 / 3
x + 2 = 8
x = 8 – 2
x = 6

37. B
My age: x

My brother is 3 years older than me: x + 3

My father is 3 less than 2 times my age: 2x – 3

My father's age divided by 5 is equal to my brother's age divided by 3: (2x – 3) / 5 = (x + 3) / 3
By cross multiplication: 5(x + 3) = 3(2x – 3)

5x + 15 = 6x – 9
x = 24

My father's age: 2.24 – 3= 48 – 3 = 45

38. C
There are two fractions containing x and the denominators are different. First, find a common denominator to simplify the expression. The least common multiplier of 4 and 7 is 28. Then,

$7(x - 2) / 28 - 4(3x + 5) / 28 = -3.28 / 28$ ... Since both sides are written on the denominator 28 now, we can eliminate them:

$7(x - 2) - 4(3x + 5) = -84$

$7x - 14 - 12x - 20 = -84$
$-5x = -84 + 14 + 20$
$-5x = -50$
$x = 50/5$
$x = 10$

39. C
The inner angles of a triangle sum up to 180°. Let us sum three expressions given for the inner angles equating to 180° and then find x:

$(x + 20) + (3x - 10) + (8x + 50) = 180$
$x + 3x + 8x + 20 - 10 + 50 = 180$
$12x + 60 = 180$
$12x = 120$
$x = 10$

Without calculation, it is obvious that 8x + 50 is the largest angle, but we cannot know which of the remaining two expressions gives the smallest value; so calculate each:

$x + 20 = 10 + 20 = 30$
$3x - 10 = 30 - 10 = 20$
$8x + 50 = 80 + 50 = 130$

The largest angle is 130° and the smallest is 20°. Their difference is 130 − 20 = 110°.

40. B
The width of the rectangle is given to be two thirds of the length. So, if we call the length by a, the width should be (2/3)a. To deal with fractions, let us say that:

length = 3x

Then, width = (2/3)3x = 2x

Remember that the perimeter of a rectangle is found by summing all sides, which means summing two lengths and two widths.

Perimeter = 2.3x + 2.2x = 150
6x + 4x = 150
10x = 150
x = 15

We are asked to find the length, that is
3x = 3.15 = 45 cm.

41. D
The volume of a sphere is found by $V_{sphere} = (4/3)\pi r^3$

The volume of a cylinder is found by $V = \pi r^2 h$ ... In the question, the radius of the cylinder is 3r. Then,
$V_{cylinder} = \pi(3r)^2 h = 9\pi r^2 h$

Since in this question $V_{sphere} = V_{cylinder}$,

$(4/3)\pi r^3 = 9\pi r^2 h$ ... Eliminating πr^2 from both sides:

$(4/3)r = 9h$ ... By cross multiplication:
4r = 27h

We are asked to find r/h. From the above equation, we can say that if r = 27k, then h = 4k.

r/h = 27k / 4k = 27/4.

42. A
The area of a triangle is found by the formula
Area = (1/2) * base *height

Let us say that base = x
The height of this triangle is 4 cm less than 3 times the base; so, height = 3x − 4

Applying these to the equation above:

Area = 32 = (1/2) * x * (3x − 4)
By cross multiplication and distributing the parenthesis,

64 = 3x² − 4x
3x² − 4x − 64 = 0 ... By factorization,

3x   −16

x   4
(3x − 16)(x + 4) = 0
There are two solutions for x:

1) 3x − 16 = 0 → x = 16/3

2) x + 4 = 0 → x = -4 ... Since a length measure cannot be negative, this cannot be a possible solution.

The only solution for x is 16/3.

We are asked to find the height, that is 3x − 4 = 3(16/3) − 4 = 16 − 4 = 12 cm.

43. C
Since we do not know the value of x, we do not know if 5x − 3 is negative or positive. Therefore, we need to con-

sider all possible solutions.

$5x - 3 \leq 7$ and $-(5x - 3) \leq 7$ are two possible cases. Let us organize the second one:

$-(5x - 3) \leq 7$ ... Multiply both sides by -1 and do not forget to change the direction of the inequality:

$5x - 3 \geq -7$

Now, we can combine both cases for $|5x - 3| \leq 7$:
$-7 \leq 5x - 3 \leq 7$

We are searching for a solution for x alone. Therefore, let us add 3 to all sides:

$-7 + 3 \leq 5x - 3 + 3 \leq 7 + 3$
$-4 \leq 5x \leq 10$

Now, let us divide all sides by 5:
$-4/5 \leq x \leq 2$

Integer values within this interval are 0, 1 and 2. The sum of these is $0 + 1 + 2 = 3$.

44. A
Since we do not know the value of x, we do not know if $7 - 2x$ is negative or positive. Therefore, we need to consider all possible solutions.

If $7 - 2x$ is positive, then $|7 - 2x| = 7 - 2x \rightarrow 7 - 2x = 9$
$2x = -2 \rightarrow x = -1$

If $7 - 2x$ is negative, then $|7 - 2x| = -(7 - 2x) = 2x - 7 \rightarrow 2x - 7 = 9$

$2x = 16 \rightarrow x = 8$

Multiplying the two solutions: (-1)(8) = -8.

45. A
First let us leave the absolute value alone by adding -8 to both sides:

$|x - 5| + 8 - 8 < 4 - 8$

$|x - 5| < -4$

This inequality tells that the result of the absolute value is negative and is smaller than -4. However, the result of an absolute value can be zero the smallest; it cannot be a negative number. Then in this question, there is no solution for the inequality given.

Next Level Logic: Advanced Algebra & Functions

Advanced Algebra

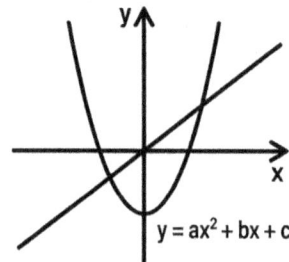

Advanced Algebra

The Advanced Algebra section covers the following:

Trigonometry
Sequences
Logarithms

Advanced Algebra

Trigonometry - A Quick Tutorial

If we are observing a right triangle, where a and b are its legs and c is its hypotenuse, we can use trigonometric functions to make a relationship between angles and sides of the right triangle.

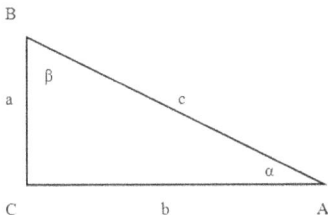

If the right angle of the right triangle ABC is at the point C, then the sine (sin) and the cosine (cos) of the angles α (at the point A) and β (at the point B) can be found like this:

$$\sin\alpha = a/c \quad \sin\beta = b/c$$
$$\cos\alpha = b/c \quad \cos\beta = a/c$$

Notice that sinα and cosβ are the equal, and same goes for sinβ and cosα. So, to find sine of the angle, we divide the side that is opposite of that angle and the hypotenuse. To find cosine of the angle, we divide the side that makes that angle (adjacent side) by the hypotenuse.

There are 2 more important trigonometric functions, tangent and cotangent:

$$tg\alpha = \sin\alpha/\cos\alpha = a/b$$
$$ctg\alpha = \cos\alpha/\sin\alpha = b/a$$

For the functions sine and cosine, there is a table with values for some of the angles, which is to be memorized as it is very useful for solving various trigonometric problems.

	0°	30°	45°	60°	90°
sinα	0	1/2	√2/2	√3/2	1
cosα	1	√3/2	√2/2	1/2	0

Let's see an example:

If a is 9 cm and c is 18 cm, find α.
We can use the sine for this problem:
$$\sin\alpha = a/c = 9/18 = 1/2$$

We can see from the table that if sinα is 1/2, then angle α is 30°.

Besides degrees we can write angles using π, where π represents 180°. For example, angle π/2 means a right angle of 90°.

Logarithms - A Quick Tutorial

Logarithm is a function that has the form

$$\log_y x = a$$

Advanced Algebra

It actually solves this equation: which number do we put as a degree on the variable y to get the variable x, that is:

$$y^a = x$$

y is called the base and a is the exponent.
For example, let's solve logarithm $\log_5 25 = a$.

$$5^a = 25$$
$$5^a = 5^2$$
$$a = 2$$

Here, we represent 25 using 5 and the second degree. a and 2 are both on the number 5, so they must be the same.

We can see from the way the logarithm works, that:

$$\log_a 1 = 0 \text{ and } \log_a a = 1$$

From $\log_a 1 = 0$ we have that $a^0 = 1$, which is true for any real number a.

From $\log_a a = 1$ we have that $a^1 = a$, which is true for any real number a.

If in the logarithm the base is 10, then instead of $\log_{10}$ we write l_g.

When we are solving some logarithm, any part can be unknown. In the first example, we had a case where the exponent was the unknown variable. Let's see another example, where both exponent and base are known:

$\log_g x = 2$
$10^2 = x$
$x = 100$

Sequences - A Quick Tutorial

A sequence of numbers is a set of numbers, but here they are in order. For example, we can represent the set of natural numbers N as a sequence 1, 2, 3,... A sequence can be finite or infinite. In our case of the sequence of the natural numbers, we have an infinite sequence.

If we have a sequence of numbers a_1, a_2, a_3,... we denote that sequence by $\{a_n\}$. We can write, for example, the sequence of natural numbers like this:

$$a_n = a_{n-1} + 1 \quad \text{or} \quad a_{n+1} = a_n + 1$$

From this formula, we can see that each number is greater than the previous number by one, which is true for the sequence of the natural numbers.

The first term (member) of the sequence is denoted by a0. So, if we know the first term of the sequence, and we know the formula that describes the sequence, we can find any term of that sequence. Even if we know some other member of the sequence, we can find other members.

Let's solve 2 examples for both cases:

1) If $a_0 = 2$ and $a_n = a_{n-1} - 2$, find the 4th member of the sequence $\{a_n\}$.

Let's find 2nd and 3rd member, which we will use to find the 4th.

$$a_1 = a_0 - 2 = 2 - 2 = 0$$
$$a_2 = a_1 - 2 = 0 - 2 = -2$$
$$a_3 = a_2 - 2 = -2 - 2 = -4$$

So, our 4th member is number -4.

2) If $a_2 = 4$ and $a_n = 2a_{n-1}$, find the 1st member of the sequence $\{a_n\}$.

$$a_2 = 2a_1 \rightarrow 4 = 2a_1 \rightarrow a_1 = 2$$
$$a_1 = 2a_0 \rightarrow 2 = 2a_0 \rightarrow a_0 = 1$$

So, our first member is 1.

ACCUPLACER® Math Practice

Answer Sheet

1. Ⓐ Ⓑ Ⓒ Ⓓ   21. Ⓐ Ⓑ Ⓒ Ⓓ
2. Ⓐ Ⓑ Ⓒ Ⓓ   22. Ⓐ Ⓑ Ⓒ Ⓓ
3. Ⓐ Ⓑ Ⓒ Ⓓ   23. Ⓐ Ⓑ Ⓒ Ⓓ
4. Ⓐ Ⓑ Ⓒ Ⓓ   24. Ⓐ Ⓑ Ⓒ Ⓓ
5. Ⓐ Ⓑ Ⓒ Ⓓ   25. Ⓐ Ⓑ Ⓒ Ⓓ
6. Ⓐ Ⓑ Ⓒ Ⓓ   26. Ⓐ Ⓑ Ⓒ Ⓓ
7. Ⓐ Ⓑ Ⓒ Ⓓ   27. Ⓐ Ⓑ Ⓒ Ⓓ
8. Ⓐ Ⓑ Ⓒ Ⓓ   28. Ⓐ Ⓑ Ⓒ Ⓓ
9. Ⓐ Ⓑ Ⓒ Ⓓ   29. Ⓐ Ⓑ Ⓒ Ⓓ
10. Ⓐ Ⓑ Ⓒ Ⓓ   30. Ⓐ Ⓑ Ⓒ Ⓓ
11. Ⓐ Ⓑ Ⓒ Ⓓ   31. Ⓐ Ⓑ Ⓒ Ⓓ
12. Ⓐ Ⓑ Ⓒ Ⓓ   32. Ⓐ Ⓑ Ⓒ Ⓓ
13. Ⓐ Ⓑ Ⓒ Ⓓ   33. Ⓐ Ⓑ Ⓒ Ⓓ
14. Ⓐ Ⓑ Ⓒ Ⓓ   34. Ⓐ Ⓑ Ⓒ Ⓓ
15. Ⓐ Ⓑ Ⓒ Ⓓ   35. Ⓐ Ⓑ Ⓒ Ⓓ
16. Ⓐ Ⓑ Ⓒ Ⓓ   36. Ⓐ Ⓑ Ⓒ Ⓓ
17. Ⓐ Ⓑ Ⓒ Ⓓ   37. Ⓐ Ⓑ Ⓒ Ⓓ
18. Ⓐ Ⓑ Ⓒ Ⓓ   38. Ⓐ Ⓑ Ⓒ Ⓓ
19. Ⓐ Ⓑ Ⓒ Ⓓ   39. Ⓐ Ⓑ Ⓒ Ⓓ
20. Ⓐ Ⓑ Ⓒ Ⓓ   40. Ⓐ Ⓑ Ⓒ Ⓓ

Advanced Algebra Practice

1. If sides a and b of a right triangle are 8 and 6, respectively, find cosine of α.

    a. 1/5
    b. 5/3
    c. 3/5
    d. 2/5

2. Find tangent of α of a right triangle, if a is 3 and b is 5.

    a. 1/4
    b. 5/3
    c. C. 4/3
    d. d. 3/4

3. If α = 30°, find sin30° + cos60°.

    a. 1/2
    b. 2/3
    c. 1
    d. 3/2

4. Calculate (sin230° - sin0°) / (cos90° - cos60°).

    a. -1/2
    b. 2/3
    c. 0
    d. 1/2

ACCUPLACER® Math Practice

5. Find cotangent of a right angle.

   a. -1
   b. 0
   c. 1/2
   d. -1/2

6. For any α, find tgα / ctgα.

   a. -1
   b. 0
   c. 1/2
   d. 1

7. Calculate (cos(π/2) + ctg(π/2)) / sin(π/2).

   a. -2
   b. -1
   c. 0
   d. 1/2

8. If in the right triangle, a is 12 and sinα = 12/13, find cosα.

   a. -5/13
   b. -1/13
   c. 1/13
   d. 5/13

9. Using the right triangle's legs, calculate
$(\sin\alpha + \cos\beta) / (tg\alpha + ctg\beta)$.

   a. a/b
   b. b/c
   c. b/a
   d. a/c

10. What is the value of the expression
$(1 - 4\sin^2(\pi/6)) / (1 + 4\cos^2(\pi/3))$?

   a. -2
   b. -1
   c. 0
   d. 1/2

Logarithms

11. If $\log_{2x} = 3$, then x is:

   a. 9
   b. 8
   c. 7
   d. 6

12. Solve the equation $\log_4 1/4 = x$.

   a. -1
   b. 0
   c. 1
   d. 2

ACCUPLACER® Math Practice

13. For what x is the following equation correct:
    $\log_x 125 = 3$

   a. 1
   b. 2
   c. 3
   d. 5

14. Find x if $\log_x(9/25) = 2$.

   a. 3/5
   b. 5/3
   c. 6/5
   d. 5/6

15. Solve $\log_{10} 10,000 = x$.

   a. 2
   b. 4
   c. 3
   d. 6

16. Find x if $\log_{1/2} x = 4$.

   a. 16
   b. 8
   c. 1/8
   d. 1/16

17. If $2x = y$ and $\log_y 256 = x^2$, find the value of x.

   a. 1
   b. 2
   c. 3
   d. 5

— Advanced Algebra —

18. We are given that $0 \leq \log_3(x + 4) \leq 3$. Find the sum of all possible integers for x satisfying the inequality.

   a. 215
   b. 221
   c. 258
   d. 270

19. Given $g(x) = \ln x$ and $f(x) = e^x$, find $(f \circ g)(x)$.

   a. 1
   b. e
   c. x
   d. e^x

20. Given $\log_2(2x - 5) - \log_2(x + 3) = 0$, find the value of $\log_8 x$.

   a. 0
   b. 1
   c. 2
   d. 8

21. Given $\log_4 x = \log_{1/16} y$, find $\log_{1/8}(x^2 y)$.

   a. −1/3
   b. −1/2
   c. 0
   d. 1/3

22. When rounded to the nearest integer, find the value of $\log_4(2 + 4 + 6 + \ldots + 30)$.

a. 3
b. 4
c. 5
d. 6

23. Given $\ln x = 2.1$ and, find the value of $\sqrt[7]{x^5}$.

a. 1
b. e
c. $e^{1.5}$
d. 3e

24. Given $5^a = 1/2$ and $3^b = 1/25$, find $a * b$.

a. 1
b. $\log_2 3$
c. ln4
d. $\log_3 4$

25. Given $4^{a+1} - 2^{a-1} - 15 = 0$, find the value of a.

a. -15/2
b. 1
c. 2
d. 15

Sequences

26. If $a_0 = 3$ and $a_n = -a_{n-1}+3$, find a_3 of the sequence $\{a_n\}$.

    a. 0
    b. 1
    c. 2
    d. 3

27. If terms of the sequence $\{a_n\}$ are represented by $a_n = a_{n-1}/n$ and $a_1 = 1$, find a_4.

    a. 1/2
    b. 1/4
    c. 1/16
    d. 1/24

28. If $a_0 = 1/2$ and $a_n = 2\, a_{n-1}^2$, find a_2 of the sequence $\{a_n\}$.

    a. 1/2
    b. 1/4
    c. 1/16
    d. 1/24

29. If members of the sequence $\{a_n\}$ are represented by $a_n = (-1)^n\, a_{n-1}$ and if $a_2 = 2$, find a_0.

    a. 2
    b. 1
    c. 0
    d. -2

30. If the sequence $\{a_n\}$ is defined by $a_{n+1} = 1 - a_n$ and $a_2 = 6$, find a_4.

a. 2
b. 1
c. 6
d. -1

31. If members of the sequence $\{a_n\}$ are represented by $a_{n+1} = -a_{n-1}$ and $a_2 = 3$ and, find $a_3 + a_4$.

a. 2
b. 3
c. 0
d. -2

32. The fundamental term of a series is $a_n = ((4 - n)/n) \cdot a_{n-1}$. If $a_1 = 2$, find the value of a_5.

a. 0
b. 2
c. 4
d. 6

33. Given $a_{n+2} = a_{n+1} * a_n$ and $a5 = 3$, find the value of $a_3 * a_6$.

a. 3
b. 5
c. 9
d. 15

34. The first three terms of a geometric sequence are (a-1), (3a+1) and (9a+19). Find the fourth term of this sequence.

   a. 112
   b. 243
   c. 256
   d. 558

35. The sum of first n terms of a series is $2n^2 - 1$. What is the eighth term of this series?

   a. 12
   b. 30
   c. 63
   d. 125

36. The fundamental term of a series is an = $n! * 3^{n-1}$. Find a_{n+4}/a_{n+2}.

   a. $n^2 + 63n + 48$
   b. $3n^2 + 6n + 48$
   c. $3n^2 + 3n + 68$
   d. $9n^2 + 63n + 108$

37. $a_n = a_{N-2} / 6$ and $a_1 = 4$ are given. What is the expression for a_{101}?

   a. $4/6^{50}$
   b. $4/6!$
   c. $4/6^{50!}$
   d. $4/6!^{50}$

ACCUPLACER® Math Practice

38. Which one of the series below is not a constant series?

    a. $a_n = (2n+4)/(5n+10)$
    b. $b_n = \cos(2n\pi)$
    c. $c_n = \sin((n+1/2)\pi)$
    d. $d_n = 9$

39. Given $a_n = (n+5)/(n+4)$, what is the multiplication of the first 200 terms of the sequence?

    a. 41
    b. 54
    c. 78
    d. 92

40. We are given that $a_{n+1} = a_n + n$ and $a_1 = 3$. Find a_{53}.

    a. 987
    b. 1102
    c. 1381
    d. 1561

Answer Key

Trigonometry

1. C
$a = 8$
$b = 6$
$a^2 + b^2 = c^2$
$8^2 + 6^2 = c^2$
$64 + 36 = c^2$
$c^2 = 100$
$c = 10$
$\cos\alpha = b/c = 6/10 = 3/5$

2. D
$a = 3$
$c = 5$
$a^2 + b^2 = c^2$
$3^2 + b^2 = 5^2$
$b^2 = 25 - 9$
$b^2 = 16$
$b = 4$
$\mathrm{tg}\,\alpha = a/b = 3/4$

3. C
$\alpha = 30°$
$\sin 30° + \cos 60° = 1/2 + 1/2 = 1$

4. A
$(\sin 230° - \sin 0°) / (\cos 90° - \cos 60°)$
$= ((1/2)2 - 0) / (0 - 1/2)$
$= (1/4) / (-1/2) = -1/2$

5. B
$\alpha = 90°$
$\mathrm{ctg}\,90° = \cos 90° / \sin 90° = 0/1 = 0$

6. D
tgα/ctgα = (sinα/cosα) / (cosα/sinα) = 1
or

tgα/ctgα = (a/b) / (b/a) = ab/ab = 1

7. C
(cos(π/2) + ctg(π/2)) / sin(π/2)
= (cos90° + ctg90°) / sin90° = (0 + 0)/1 = 0

8. D
a = 12
sinα = 12/13 = a/c
a/c = 12/13
12/c = 12/13
c = 13

$a^2 + b^2 = c^2$
$12^2 + b^2 = 13^2$
$b^2 = 169 - 144$
$b^2 = 25$
b = 5
cosα = b/c = 5/13

9. B
(sinα + cosβ) / (tgα+ctgβ)
= (a/c + a/c) / (a/b + a/b)
=(2a/c)/(2a/b) = b/c

10. C
$(1-4\sin^2(π/6)) / (1 + 4\cos^2(π/3))$
=(1 - 4sin²(30°)) / (1 + 4cos²(60°))
=(1 - 4(1/2)²) / (1 + 4(1/2)²)
=(1 - 4(1/4)) / (1 + 4(1/4))
=(1 - 1) / (1 + 1) = 0/2 = 0

Advanced Algebra

Logarithms

11. B
$\log_2 x = 3$
$2^3 = x$
$x = 8$

12. A
$\log_4 1/4 = x.$
$4^x = 1/4$
$4^x = 4^{-1}$
$x = -1$

13. D
$\log_x 125 = 3$
$x^3 = 125$
$x^3 = 5^3$
$x = 5$

14. A
$\log_x(9/25) = 2$
$x^2 = 9/25$
$x^2 = (3/5)2$
$x = 3/5$

15. B
$\log_{10} 10{,}000 = x$
$10^x = 10{,}000$
$10^x = 10^4$
$x = 4$

16. D
$\log_{1/2} x = 4$
$(1/2)^4 = x$
$x = 1/16$

ACCUPLACER® Math Practice

17. B
We are given two equations each one containing two unknown values x and y. Then, we can extract the value of y depending on x from one equation and insert it into the other equation obtaining an equation depending only on x and so we can reach the value of x. It is clear that the first equation directly gives the value of y depending on x; therefore, let us insert this value into the second equation:

Inserting $y = 2^x$ into $\log_y 256 = x^2$:

$\log_{2^x} 256 = x^2$

Recall that $\log_a a^b = \log_a a \cdot b = b$ since $\log_a a = 1$. Then, since the base of this logarithm is 2^x, we can try to write 256 on base 2^x:

$256 = 2^8$ ... So, we need to write 2^8 in the form of 2^x. We can simply conclude that $2^8 = (2^x)^{8/x}$. Then,
$\log_{2^x} 2^8 = x^2$

$\log_{2^x} 2^{x(8/x)} = x^2$

$8/x = x^2$ ... We obtain a simple equation depending only on variable x. By cross multiplication:
$8 = x^3$
$x = 2$

18. D
We know that $0 \leq \log_3(x+4) \leq 3$. Our aim is to obtain an inequality depending on x. Therefore, we perform operations to have x alone. First, remove the logarithm on base 3.

Recall that $a^{\log_a x} = x$:

$0 \leq \log_3(x+4) \leq 3$ ... Make all sides the power of 3. This does not change the direction of the inequality:

$3^0 \leq 3^{\log_3(x+4)} \leq 3^3$ ... Recall that $c^0 = 1$:

$1 \leq x + 4 \leq 27$ ... Now, we can simply have x in the middle by subtracting 4 from all sides:

$1 - 4 \leq x + 4 - 4 \leq 27 - 4$

$-3 \leq x \leq 23$

Values within this interval satisfy the inequality. Let us sum all integers within the interval [-3, 23]. Simply, the sum of numbers from 1 up to 23 is found by: 23*24 / 2 = 276.

Then, the overall sum is:

$-3 - 2 - 1 + 0 + 276 = 270$.

19. C
To solve this problem, we need to remember the properties of composite function. (fog)(x) means that we are asked to insert function g into f; in other words, (fog)(x) = f(g(x)). We insert function g into x inside f. Here; g(x)=lnx and f(x)=e^x are given. Then,

(fog)(x)=f(g(x))=$e^{g(x)}$=$e^{\ln x}$

Recall that $a^{\log_a x}=x$ and $\ln x=\log_e x$:

(fog)(x)=$e^{\log_e x}$=x

20. B
The given equation contains only one variable that is x. Solve it by using logarithmic function properties.

$\log_2(2x-5) - \log_2(x+3) = 0$ ... Notice that both logarithms are on the same base.

Recall that $\log_a(x/y) = \log_a x - \log_a y$. Then,
$\log_2((2x-5)/(x+3)) = 0$

Remember that $\log_a a^0 = 0$:

$\log_2((2x-5)/(x+3)) = \log_2 2^0$

Since both sides are on the same logarithmic base, we can equate $((2x-5)/(x+3)) = 2^0$

$2^0 = 1$ $(2x-5)/(x+3) = 1$

By cross multiplication: $2x - 5 = x + 3$
$2x - x = 3 + 5$
$x = 8$
We are asked to find $\log_8 x$, that is $\log_8 8 = 1$.

21. C
We are given one equation containing two variables x and y and asked to find the value of a logarithmic function depending on both. This means that we will not find the values of x and y separately; but we will find a combined data based on two; we tend to find the multiplication of x^2 and y.

$\log_4 x = \log_{1/16} y$ ... Recall that $\log_{1/a} b = \log_{a^{-1}} b = -\log_a b$

$\log_4 x = -\log_{16} y$

$\log_4 x + \log_{16} y = 0$ ... to make all bases the same, we need to convert base 16 to base 4.

Remember that $\log_a b = \log_c b / \log_c a$ → $\log_{16} y = \log_4 y / \log_4 16$

$\log_4 x + \log_4 y / \log_4 4^2 = 0$ ... Remember that $\log_a a^x = x\log_a a$

$= x \cdot 1 = x$

$\log_4 x + \log_4 y / 2 = 0$

Organize the equation by multiplying both sides by 2:

$2\log_4 x + \log_4 y = 0$ ... Notice that factor 2 is the power of x:

$\log_4 x^2 + \log_4 y = 0$ ... Using the property $\log a + \log b = \log(a \cdot b)$,

$\log_4(x^2 y) = 0$

$x^2 y = 4^0 = 1$

$x^2 y = 1$ ... Now, we can calculate the value of the function given:

$\log_{1/8}(x^2 y) = -\log_8(x^2 y)$

$= -\log_8 1$
$= -\log_8 8^0$
$= 0$

22. B
Organize the number part and then apply the logarithm:
$2 + 4 + 6 + ... + 30 = 2(1 + 2 + 3 + ... + 15)$ ... Remember that the sum of integers from 1 to n is found by the formula $n(n + 1)/2$:

$= 2 \cdot (15 \cdot 16 / 2)$
$= 15 \cdot 16$

There is no need to calculate the result, this factors may be useful while applying the logarithm. Using the property $\log(a \cdot b) = \log_a + \log_b$:

$\log_4(15 \cdot 16) = \log_4 15 + \log_4 16$

$= \log_4 15 + \log_4 4^2$ ... Remember that $\log_a a^x = x\log_a a = x \cdot 1 = x$

$= \log_4 15 + 2$

Notice that $4^1 = 4$ and $4^2 = 16$; 15 is in between these two numbers.

$4 < 15 < 16$
$4^1 < 4^a < 4^2$

Then, a is between 1 and 2, closer to 2. Since 15 is close to 16 rather than 4, a is closer to 2 rather than 1.
Then;
$\log_4 15 \sim 2 \rightarrow \log_4(2 + 4 + 6 + ... + 30) \sim 2 + 2 = 4$.

23. C
We have an equation giving information on x and we are asked to find the value of a term containing x. Then, we will use the first data to obtain the result.

$\sqrt[7]{x^5} = x^{5/7}$ ... Let us name this term by "t":

$t = x^{5/7}$ ... Taking logarithm of both sides on natural base e ($\log_e x$ means lnx):

$lnt = lnx^{5/7}$ ... Remember that $\log a^x = x\log a$:

$lnt = (5/7)lnx$ ... Inserting the value of lnx which is given in the question:

$lnt = (5/7) \cdot 2.1$ ... Simplifying 2.1 by 7:
$lnt = 5 \cdot 0.3$

Int = 1.5 ... Since $a^{\log_a x} = x$, let us make both sides the power of e to obtain t alone:

$e^{\text{Int}} = e^{1.5}$
$t = e^{1.5}$
$t = x^{5/7} = e^{1.5}$

24. D
Having two equations and two unknowns a and b, let us find their values first and then multiply.

$5^a = 1/2$ ... Applying logarithm to both sides on base 5:
$\log_5 5^a = \log_5(1/2)$ ... Remember that $\log_a a^x = x \log_a a$
$= x * 1 = x$:
$a = \log_5(1/2)$ ... Recall that $1/2 = 2^{-1}$
$a = -\log_5 2$
$3^b = 1/25$ ... Applying logarithm to both sides on base 3:

$\log_3 3^b = \log_3(1/25)$ ... Remember that $\log_a a^x = x \log_a a = x \cdot 1$
$= x$:

$b = \log_3(1/25)$ ... Recall that $1/25 = 1/5^2 = 5^{-2}$
$b = -2\log_3 5$

We are asked to find a·b:

$a \cdot b = (-\log_5 2)(-2\log_3 5)$

$= 2 \log_5 2 \cdot \log_3 5$ ... Recall that $\log_a b = \log_c b / \log_c a$ is used to change base:

$= 2 \cdot (\log_3 2 / \log_3 5) \cdot \log_3 5$ ... $\log_3 5$ terms cancel each other:
$= 2\log_3 2$
$= \log_3 2^2$
$= \log_3 4$

25. B

$4^{a+1} - 2^{a-1} - 15 = 0$ ... Notice that 4 is the second power of 2. Then, we can write both in the same form:

$2^{2a+2} - 2^a / 2 - 15 = 0$

$4 * 2^{2a} - 2^a / 2 - 15 = 0$ ... Let us apply variable change $2^a = t$ to obtain a quadratic form:

$4t^2 - t/2 - 15 = 0$ ... Multiply both sides by 2:

$8t^2 - t - 30 = 0$ ... By factorization, we have:

$(8t + 15)(t - 2) = 0$ ... There are two solutions for t:

1) $8t + 15 = 0 \rightarrow t = -15/2 \rightarrow 2^a = -15/2$ ... Since an exponential cannot have a negative value, this is not a valid result; we need to eliminate this.

2) $t - 2 = 0 \rightarrow t = 2 \rightarrow 2^a = 2 \quad 2^a = 2^1 \rightarrow a = 1$ ... This is the only solution for a.

Sequences

26. A

$a_0 = 3$
$a_n = -a_{n-1} + 3$
$a_1 = -a_{0+3} = -3 + 3 = 0$
$a_2 = -a_{1+3} = 0 + 3 = 3$
$a_3 = -a_{2+3} = -3 + 3 = 0$

27. D

$a_n = a_{n-1}/n$
$a_1 = 1$
$a_2 = a_1/2 = 1/2$
$a_3 = a_2/3 = (1/2)/3 = 1/6$
$a_4 = a_3/4 = (1/6)/4 = 1/24$

Advanced Algebra

28. A
$a_0 = 1/2$
$a_n = 2a_{n-1}^2$
$a_1 = 2a_0^2 = 2 \cdot (1/2)^2 = 2 \cdot (1/4) = 1/2$
$a_2 = 2a_1^2 = 2 \cdot (1/2)^2 = 2 \cdot (1/4) = 1/2$

29. D
$a_n = (-1)^n a_{n-1}$
$a_2 = 2$
$2 = a_2 = (-1)^2 a_1 = a_1 \rightarrow a_1 = 2$
$a_1 = (-1)^1 a_0$
$2 = -a_0$
$a_0 = -2$

30. C
$a_{n+1} = 1 - a_n$
$a_2 = 6$
$a_3 = 1 - a_2 = 1 - 6 = -5$
$a_4 = 1 - a_3 = 1 - (-5) = 1 + 5 = 6$

31. C
$a_{n+1} = -a_{n-1}$
$a_2 = 3$
$a_3 = -a_2 = -3$
$a_4 = -a_3 = -(-3) = 3$
$a_3 + a_4 = -3 + 3 = 0$

32. A
$a_n = ((4-n)/n) a_{n-1}$ ... The fundamental term of the series tells that, any term in the series depends on the term prior to itself. Then, we can start inserting 2 for n and continuing up to n = 5 to find the value of a_5.

$n = 2$: $a_2 = ((4-2)/2) a_1 = (2/2) 2 = 2$

$n = 3$: $a_3 = ((4-3)/3) a_2 = (1/3) 2 = 2/3$

$n = 4$: $a_4 = ((4-4)/4) a_3 = (0/4)(2/3) = 0$ ... Once we see a term that is zero, we can foresee that all upcoming terms will be zero, because the fundamental term tells that a term is found by multiplying a factor by the previous term.

Zero is the absorbing element of multiplication. Since the previous term is zero, all following terms will be zero.

Though, a_5 is calculated below:

n = 5: $a_5 = ((4 - 5) / 5) a_4 = (-1/5) 0 = 0$

33. C
We need to insert different values into the equation that make it possible to obtain information on a_3, a_6 and a_5.

All three cannot exist in the same equation since a_{n+2}, a_{n+1} and a_n are consecutive numbers but a_3, a_6 and a_5 are not.

n = 3: $a_5 = a_4 \cdot a_3$

n = 4: $a_6 = a_5 \cdot a_4$

The two equations together contain a_3, a_6 and a_5 as we needed. Also, there are a_4 terms that are not needed. Let us divide the two equations side by side and eliminate a_4 terms:

$a_5 = a_4 \cdot a_3$
--- -------
$a_6 = a_5 \cdot a_4$
$a_5 = a_3$
--- ---

$a_6 = a_5$
By cross multiplication:
$(a_5)^2 = a_3 \cdot a_6$ ... We are given that $a_5 = 3$:
$a_3 \cdot a_6 = 3^2 = 9$

34. C
First, we need to find the common ratio (r) of the geometric sequence. Any term in the sequence is found by the multiplication of the previous term by the common ratio. Then,

r = (3a+1) / (a-1) and r = (9a+19) / (3a+1)

These two fractions should be equal since the common ratio is constant for a sequence.
(3a+1) / (a-1) = (9a+19) / (3a+1)
Cross multiply:
(3a+1)(3a+1) = (a-1)(9a+19)

$9a^2$ + 6a + 1 = $9a^2$ + 10a – 19 ... $9a^2$ terms on both sides cancel each other:
6a + 1 = 10a – 19
20 = 4a
a = 5

Using any of the fractions written above, we can find the value of r. Let us prefer the simpler one:

r = (3a+1) / (a-1)
r = (3·5+1) / (5-1)
r = 16/4
r = 4

This means that, a_{n+1} = $4a_n$

We are asked to find the fourth term, that is a_4=$4a_3$
a_3 = 9a+19 = 9·5+19 = 64
a_4=$4a_3$ = 4·64 = 256

35. B
Showing the sum of n series by S_n, we are given that S_n = $2n^2$ – 1.

The sum of n-1 terms is found by inserting n-1 for n in the equation above:

S_{n-1} = $2(n-1)^2$ – 1 = $2n^2$ – 4n + 2 – 1 = $2n^2$ – 4n + 1

ACCUPLACER® Math Practice

The difference between S_n and S_{n-1} is the nth term of the sequence, that is a_n:

$S_n - S_{n-1} = a_n = 2n^2 - 1 - (2n^2 - 4n + 1) = 2n^2 - 1 - 2n^2 + 4n - 1$

$a_n = 4n - 2$

The eighth term is found by just inserting 8 for n:
$a_8 = 4*8 - 2 = 30$

36. D
Using the formula of the fundamental term, we can find the expressions for a_{n+2} and a_{n+4}:

Inserting n+2 into n: $a_{n+2} = (n+2)!\, 3^{n+2-1} = (n+2)! \cdot 3^{n+1}$

Inserting n+4 into n: $a_{n+4} = (n+4)!\, 3^{n+4-1} = (n+4)! \cdot 3^{n+3}$

Let us perform the division a_{n+4}/a_{n+2}:

$a_{n+4}/a_{n+2} = ((n+4)! \cdot 3^{n+3}) / ((n+2)! \cdot 3^{n+1})$

$= ((n+4)! / (n+2)!) \cdot (3^{n+3} / 3^{n+1})$

$= ((n+4)(n+3)(n+2)! / (n+2)!) \cdot (3^{n+1}.3^2 / 3^{n+1})$ ... Simplifying;

$= (n+4)(n+3)3^2$

$= 9(n+3)(n+4)$ ... Distributing factors into the parenthesis:
$= 9n^2 + 63n + 108$

37. A
The fundamental term tells that any term in the sequence depends on the two previous term. We are given the first term and asked to find the hundred first term. Let us start inserting odd values for n until we get the point for the

value of the hundred first term:

$a_n = a_{n-2}/6$

n = 3: $a_3 = a_1/6 = 4/6$

n = 5: $a_5 = a_3/6 = 4/(6\cdot6)$

n = 7: $a_7 = a_5/6 = 4/(6\cdot6\cdot6)$

n = 9: $a_9 = a_7/6 = 4/(6\cdot6\cdot6\cdot6)$

Notice that for n = 2k+1, 4 is divided by k number of 6s.

Then, we can conclude that:

n = 2k+1: $a_{2k+1} = 4/6^k$

n = 101 → k = 50: $a_{101} = 4/6^{50}$

38. C
A constant series consists of terms that are all equal to each other. In other words; for different values of n, we obtain the same term.
Then, let us try all series:
$a_n = (2n+4)/(5n+10)$

Let us simplify this expression:
$a_n = (2(n+2))/(5(n+2)) = 2/5$

Since we obtain a constant value, a_n series is a constant series.

$b_n = \cos(2n\pi)$

Let us insert values for n:
n = 1 → $b_1 = \cos2\pi = \cos0 = 1$
n = 2 → $b_2 = \cos4\pi = \cos0 = 1$
n = 3 → $b_3 = \cos6\pi = \cos0 = 1$

Notice that for any value of n, we obtain the cosine of even multiples of π of which cosine is always 1. This means that, b_n series is a constant series.
$c_n = \sin((n+1/2)\pi)$

Let us insert values for n:
$n = 1 \rightarrow c_1 = \sin(3\pi/2) = -1$
$n = 2 \rightarrow c_2 = \sin(5\pi/2) = 1$
$n = 3 \rightarrow c_3 = \sin(7\pi/2) = -1$
$n = 4 \rightarrow c_4 = \sin(9\pi/2) = 1$

The unit circle is completed by n = 4 and then the same values are repeated in the series. Since the terms are different, this is not a constant series. Though, let us prove that the remaining series is constant.

$d_n = 9$

This series is obviously a constant series; 9 is independent of the value assigned to n.

39. A

The given fundamental term of the series is a fraction of which denominator and numerator are consecutive numbers. From this point, we can understand that there will be simplifications while multiplying 200 terms of the sequence.

Let us start by finding a few terms:
n = 1: $a_1 = 6/5$
n = 2: $a_2 = 7/6$
n = 3: $a_3 = 8/7$
.
.
.
n = 200: $a_{200} = 205/204$

Multiplying the 200 terms, we have:
(6/5)(7/6)(6/7) ... (205/204)

Notice that the numerator of the first term and the denominator of the second term cancel. This goes on and the denominator 204 is eliminated by the numerator of the previous term. Then, we have 205/5 left after simplification.
205/5 = 41.

40. C
Starting by n = 1, we can find the value of the upcoming term and continue until 53. However, this is a very long method. Instead, let us write expressions for some of the first terms and the 53th term lastly:

n = 1: $a_2 = a_1 + 1$
n = 2: $a_3 = a_2 + 2$
n = 3: $a_4 = a_3 + 3$
.
.
.
n = 52: $a_{53} = a_{52} + 52$

If we sum all 52 equations side-by-side, we notice that terms starting from a_2 to a_{52} cancel and we obtain:

$a_{53} = a_1 + (1 + 2 + 3 + ... + 52)$

We know that $a_1 = 3$. Also, the sum of the terms from 1 to 52 is found by: 52·53/2 = 1378.

Then,
a_{53} = 1378 + 3 = 1381.

The Kitchen Table Guide: How to Actually Study Math

How to Study for a Math Test

How to Master Accuplacer Math

Success on a high-level math placement test isn't about being a "math person." It's about recognizing that math is a language of logic. You don't study it by reading; you study it by *doing*. Here is how we recommend tackling the advanced material in this workbook.

— Basic Math Multiple Choice —

1. Close the Gaps (The "House of Cards" Principle)
Math is uniquely hierarchical. You cannot master Logarithms if your understanding of Exponents is shaky. If you find yourself "glossing over" a concept because it feels too dense, stop. That missing piece is a crack in your foundation that will cause your "math house" to topple later on.

- **Trace it back:** If an Algebra II problem stumps you, identify the specific operation (factoring, fractions, radicals) that caused the trip-up and review that basic skill first.
- **Don't skip the "Why":** At this level, don't just memorize a formula like $a^x/a^y = a^{x-y}$. Understand that you are simply cancelling out repeated factors. When you understand the *why*, you don't have to stress about the *how*.
-

2. Move Beyond Passive Review
Reading through a solved example in this book is a great start, but it's a "passive" activity. Your brain is just following a map someone else drew.

- **The "Blank Page" Test:** After looking at an example solution, cover it up. Take a fresh sheet of paper and try to solve it from scratch. If you get stuck, you haven't learned it yet—you've only recognized it.
- **Practice at the Edge:** Spend 80% of your time on the problems that make you slightly uncomfortable. Solving "easy" problems feels good, but it's just treading water. To move ahead, you have to dive into the deep end.
-

3. Build Visual and Logical Anchors

Advanced math can get abstract. Use "anchors" to keep yourself grounded.

- **Synthesize Shapes:** If you're stuck on a complex polygon, break it down into triangles. Use the properties you know (like the 180^0 rule) to conquer the unknown.
- **Create Mental Shortcuts:** For the elevator analogy mentioned earlier—changing floors (numerator to denominator) requires changing your "button" (the sign of the exponent). These small mental hooks make complex formulas stick in long-term memory.
-

4. Own Your Strategy

Every student has a "unique' way of processing logic.

- **Take Your Own Notes:** Never rely on someone else's shortcuts. Rewrite rules in your own words. If "FOIL" doesn't make sense to you, call it "Double Distribution." Whatever makes the lightbulb go off is the right way.
- **Audit Your Weaknesses:** Keep a running list of "The Big Five"—the five concepts that scare you the most. Attack those first every study session when your brain is fresh.

5. The Mental and Physical Game

The Accuplacer is a marathon, not a sprint.

- **The "1-Step" Rule:** You will hit walls. You will spend 20 minutes on a single problem and feel like you've wasted time. You haven't. That struggle is where the actual learning happens. Every mistake you catch now is a point you save on test day.

- **Conditioning:** Your brain runs on fuel. Avoid the "fast food fog" before a heavy study session. Get a solid night's sleep so your mind can move information from short-term "cram" memory into long-term "mastery" memory.

Smart Strategy: Pre-Game Prep for Success

How to Prepare for a Test

Many students freeze when faced with a major exam. It is a natural reaction to want to avoid the stress, hide your head in the sand, and hope for the best. However, avoidance is a guarantee of anxiety. The antidote to test anxiety is action.

Test preparation is not just about memorizing facts; it is about strategy, dedication, and self-discipline. These are not just academic skills—they are professional skills. The ability to set a goal, create a roadmap, and execute a plan is what will make you successful in your future career.

Below is a comprehensive guide to mastering the art of preparation.

Phase 1: The Setup

Before you open a single textbook, you must set the stage for success.

Take Ownership of Your Prep

It is a common mistake to link your studying entirely to someone else. While study groups can be beneficial for reviewing concepts, your core preparation must be a solo mission. Study partners can get sick, be distracting, or have different learning gaps than you do. It is your job to be prepared, regardless of what others are doing. Do not allow the social aspect of studying to distract you from your goals.

Optimize Your Environment

Do not try to squeeze high-quality study time into a low-quality environment. You need a dedicated "command center."

- **Find your zone:** Locate a peaceful spot with minimal distractions, such as a library, a quiet park, or a home office.
- **The Bedroom Rule:** Avoid studying on your bed. Your brain associates your bed with sleep, which can lead to drowsiness. Conversely, if you stress over books in bed, you may find it harder to sleep at night. Keep your rest zone and your work zone separate.
- **Ergonomics:** Ensure you have good lighting, a comfortable chair, and a desk surface large enough to spread out your materials.

Gather Your "Intel"

Nothing breaks a study flow faster than searching for a missing highlighter or realizing you lost your notes. Before you begin, gather:

- Textbooks, notebooks, and class slides.
- Laptop and charger.
- Stationery (pens, pencils, highlighters, sticky notes).
- Hydration and healthy snacks (brain food).
- Phone Management: Keep your phone with you if you need it for research, but place it in "Do Not Disturb" mode. One notification can break 20 minutes of focus.

Phase 2: The Study Strategy

Passive reading is not studying. To retain information, you must be active.

Master Your Schedule

Analyze your biological clock. Are you a morning lark or a night owl? Schedule your most difficult topics for the time of day when your brain is sharpest.

- **The Chunking Method:** Most brains cannot handle 4 hours of relentless focus. Break your time into blocks (e.g., 50 minutes of study, 10 minutes of break).
- **The "Gap" Strategy:** Use flashcards for "gap times"—waiting for the bus, standing in line, or during commercial breaks. While deep study requires a desk, reviewing terminology can happen anywhere.

Active Review Techniques

Don't just read your notes; interact with them.

- **Rewrite to Remember:** Re-writing your notes summarizes the information and forces your brain to process it again.

- **Teacher Mode:** Try to explain a complex concept out loud, as if you were teaching it to someone else. If you stumble, you don't know it well enough yet.

- **Prioritize Class Notes:** Pay special attention to comments made by the instructor or topics emphasized in class. If the teacher spent 20 minutes on a slide, it will likely be on the test.

Assess Your Weaknesses

You cannot fix what you do not know is broken. Early in your preparation, take a diagnostic or practice test to identify your "red zones"—the areas where you struggle the most.

- Spend 70% of your time on your weak areas.
- Spend 30% of your time maintaining your strong areas.

Resource Tip: Look online for additional assessment tools. Visit our website at https://www.test-preparation.ca for test tips, practice questions, and study guides designed to help you identify your strengths and weaknesses.

Phase 3: Mental and Physical Readiness

Your brain is an organ. It needs care, and your mindset dictates your performance.

The Anti-Procrastination Rule

Procrastination is the enemy of confidence. Cramming the night before increases cortisol (stress hormone) levels, which actually blocks memory retrieval.

- **Start Early:** Reviewing material in small chunks over two weeks is far more effective than studying for 8 hours straight the day before.

- **Avoid the Spiral:** When you procrastinate, you start telling yourself, "I can't learn this in time." This negative self-talk becomes a self-fulfilling prophecy.

Psych Yourself Up (Not Out)

- **Positive Self-Talk:** It sounds simple, but it works. Replace "I hope I don't fail" with "I have prepared, and I am ready." Positive internal dialogue drowns out anxiety.

- **Visualization:** Athletes use this technique, and so should you. Close your eyes and visualize the test environment. See yourself calm, flipping the page, recognizing the questions, and writing the answers with confidence.

- **Stay in Your Lane:** Do not compare yourself to other students. You don't know if they are actually prepared or just acting confident. Their performance has zero impact on your grade. Focus entirely on your own progress.

Protect Your Headspace

Worry is contagious. In the days leading up to the test, avoid classmates who are panicking or complaining about how hard the test will be. Even if you are prepared, their anxiety can "infect" you. Isolate yourself from negativity and trust in the work you have done.

By combining a solid study environment, active learning strategies, and a positive mindset, you are doing more than just studying for a test—you are training yourself to succeed.

How to Prepare for a Test - The Ultimate Guide

https://www.test-preparation.ca/prepare-test/

How to Study - The Ultimate Guide

https://test-preparation.ca/learning-study/

Test-Day Tactics: Staying Sharp Under Pressure

How to Take a Test

Master the Exam – Strategies for Test Day

You have done the preparation. You have put in the study hours. Now, you are in the exam room. This phase requires a shift in mindset from "learning" to "executing."

Taking a test is a skill in itself. A student with average knowledge but excellent test-taking strategies will often outperform a student with superior knowledge but poor strategy. Below is a tactical guide to maximizing your score while the clock is ticking.

How to Take a Test

Phase 1: The Arrival and Setup

The test begins before the timer starts. Your goal upon arrival is to minimize stress and eliminate distractions.

Arrive Early (But Not Too Early)

Rushing spikes your adrenaline and clouds your thinking. Arrive early enough to find the room, visit the restroom, and settle in. However, avoid arriving so early that you sit for an hour absorbing the anxiety of other nervous students.

- **Ignore the Noise:** Do not chat with friends about what they studied or what they "heard" will be on the test. This chitchat breeds doubt. Be polite, but keep your distance.

- **Climate Control:** Exam rooms are notorious for being too hot or too cold. Dress in layers so you can adjust your comfort level without being distracted.

The "Brain Dump" Technique

This is one of the most effective strategies for reducing anxiety. Unless the exam strictly forbids scratch paper, use the first two minutes of the test to "dump" information. As soon as you are allowed to write, jot down the formulas, dates, acronyms, or key facts you are afraid of forgetting.

- **Why this works:** Once the information is on the paper, you no longer have to hold it in your working memory. You can relax, knowing the information is safe and ready when you need it.

ACCUPLACER® Math Practice

Physical Relaxation

If you feel your muscles tensing up while waiting for the test to begin, try the Tense and Release method:

1. Tense your muscles tightly (clench fists, tighten shoulders, squeeze legs) for 5 seconds.
2. Release everything instantly.
3. Feel the tension leave your body.
4. Take three deep, slow breaths.

Phase 2: The Launch

Do not dive into Question 1 immediately. Take 60 seconds to strategize.

Read the Instructions... Twice

This sounds obvious, but it is the most common reason for preventable errors.

- **Check for specific rules** (e.g., "Select ALL that apply" vs. "Select the BEST answer").

- **Check the scoring policy.** Does the test penalize for wrong answers? If not, never leave a question blank. If you don't know the answer, guess.

- **If you are confused** by a sample question or instruction, ask the proctor immediately.

Scan and Budget

Briefly flip through the exam (or click through the sections if on a computer) to gauge the layout.

- **Speed vs. Accuracy:** Determine if the test is a sprint (many easy questions) or a marathon (fewer, complex questions).

- **The Time Budget:** If you have 60 minutes for 60 questions, you have one minute per question. Check the clock at the halfway mark (30 minutes) to ensure you are halfway through the questions.

- **Note on Watches:** Do not obsessively watch the clock. It increases anxiety. Check the time only at specific milestones (e.g., after every 10 questions).

Phase 3: Answering Strategies

Use these tactical approaches to handle the questions efficiently.

The "Easy First" Strategy

Do not take the test in the order it is written if you don't have to.

1. Scan for the easy wins: Go through a section and answer every question you know immediately.

2. Skip the struggle: If a question takes more than a minute, mark it and move on.

3. Return with confidence: Once you have banked all the easy points, return to the difficult questions.

- **Benefit:** This builds confidence, warms up your brain, and ensures you don't run out of time on questions you knew the answers to.

Decoding the Question

- **Circle Keywords:** Physically circle words like "NOT," "EXCEPT," "ALWAYS," "NEVER," or "MOST." These words change the entire meaning of the question.

- **Don't Read Between the Lines:** Standardized tests are usually straightforward. Do not over-analyze or look for a trick that isn't there. The simplest interpretation is usually the correct one.

- **The "True/False" Test:** If you are confused by the options, read the question and treat every option as a True/False statement. Select the one that is "Most True."

The Power of Elimination

You do not need to know the right answer to get the point; you just need to identify the wrong ones.

1. Cross out the answers that are obviously wrong.
2. Cross out answers that are "sort of" right but not the best fit.
3. If you have eliminated two options, you have increased your odds of guessing correctly from 25% to 50%.

Handling the "Impossible" Question

If you encounter a question that makes no sense:

- **Divide and Conquer:** Break the sentence into smaller phrases. Translate complex words into simple ones.
- **Context Clues:** Look for clues elsewhere in the test. Sometimes Question 45 contains the answer to Question 12.
- **Guess and Move On:** If you are truly stuck, make an educated guess and move on. Do not let one difficult question ruin your rhythm for the next five.

Phase 4: The Review

If you finish early, do not leave. Leaving early is a missed opportunity to improve your grade.

The "Bubble Check"

If you are using a scantron sheet, do a spot check. Ensure that the answer for Question 15 is actually filled into bubble 15. A "mis-bubble" can cause a domino effect of wrong answers.

The Sanity Check

Review your math and logic. Does the answer make sense?

- **Example:** If the question asks for the speed of a car and your calculation says 4,000 mph, you have likely made a calculation error.

Second Guessing

A common question students ask is: "Should I change my answer?"

- **Rule of Thumb:** Only change your answer if you have found a specific reason why your first answer was wrong (e.g., you misread the question or made a calculation error). If it is just a vague feeling of doubt, stick with your gut. Your first instinct is usually correct.

Summary Checklist

- ✓ Bring: ID, pencils, allowed materials (calculator), layers of clothing.
- ✓ Start: Brain dump formulas, read instructions carefully.
- ✓ During: Skip hard questions, circle keywords, use elimination.
- ✓ End: Review answers, check bubbles, use every allotted minute.

You have the knowledge. Now, use these strategies to ensure that the test accurately reflects what you know. Stay calm, stay focused, and go for it!

Common Accuplacer Pitfalls (And How to Dodge Them)

We've all been there. You walk out of a testing center, the adrenaline fades, and suddenly you realize you made a "silly" mistake that had nothing to do with your math skills. On the Accuplacer, those mistakes can land you in a remedial class you don't actually need.
Here is how to stay sharp:

1. The "Mis-Click" Trap
On a paper test, you might circle 'C'. On a screen, it's all about the mouse. It sounds basic, but in the heat of the moment, it's easy to solve a complex equation, find that the answer is $x = 12$, and then accidentally click the bubble for $x = 21$ because you were already thinking about the next problem.

- **The Fix:** Before you hit "Next" or "Submit," take one second to look at your scratch pad and then look at the screen. Confirm the numbers match.

2. Double-Answering (and "No-Answering")
Most digital platforms won't let you select two bubbles, but they *will* let you leave a question blank if you aren't careful. Because the Accuplacer is often adaptive, your performance on the current question determines the difficulty of the next one.

- **The Fix:** Treat every click like it's final. Ensure you haven't accidentally left a question "in limbo" before trying to move forward.

3. The Scratch Pad "Translation" Error

This is where most students lose points. You do the heavy lifting—the long division, the factoring, the multi-step algebra—on your scratch paper. But then, you misread your own handwriting when looking back at the screen.

- **The Fix:** Keep your scratch pad organized. If you're working on Question 5, label it "Q5" and circle your final result. It prevents "number bleed" where a digit from a previous problem wanders into your current calculation.

4. Mishandling the "Hard" Questions

On the Accuplacer, you often **cannot go back** to a previous question once you've submitted it. This is a huge shift from traditional tests.

- **The Strategy:** If you hit a wall, don't panic and "rage-click" a random answer just to get it over with. Take a breath, use your scratch paper to eliminate the obviously wrong choices, and make an educated guess. Since there's no penalty for guessing, a "smart guess" is always better than a blank screen.

5. Over-Thinking (The "Second-Guess" Spiral)

In Victoria, we call this "getting in your own way." Often, your first instinct is based on all those hours of practice stored in your subconscious. If you find yourself staring at a screen for five minutes, debating between two similar-looking answers and feeling your heart rate climb, you're over-thinking.

- **The Fix:** Trust your preparation. If you've done the work in this workbook, your first impulse is usually the right one. Don't let test anxiety talk you out of a correct answer.

6. Misreading the "Call" of the Question
The test-makers at "Big Prep" love to be sneaky. They'll ask for the *value of 2x*, but the first answer choice will be the *value of x*.

- **The Fix:** Always re-read the last sentence of the prompt before selecting your answer. Make sure you are actually answering what they asked, not what you *assumed* they would ask.

You've Done the Work—Now Go Own the Result

If you're reading this page, it means you've pushed through the logarithms, wrestled with the functions, and stuck with it when the mental fatigue set in. That kind of discipline is exactly what's going to make you a success in your program.

The Accuplacer is just a gatekeeper, and you've spent this time learning how to pick the lock. You've triple-checked your logic and put in the hours that most people skip. When you sit down at that computer terminal, take a deep breath and remember: you aren't guessing. You're applying everything we've worked on in these chapters.

Trust your preparation. You've got the tools; now just go use them.

Don't Head Out Just Yet—Grab Your Extras
We want to make sure you have every possible advantage before test day. If you haven't already, register your copy of this workbook. It gives you access to the "live" updates we push out, extra test-day tips, and a few more practice questions to keep your skills sharp.

Claim your free extras here:
https://www.test-preparation.ca/register/

The Toolbox: Digital Extras & Practice Portals

How to Prepare for a Test - The Ultimate Guide

https://www.test-preparation.ca/prepare-test/

Learning Styles - The Complete Guide

https://www.test-preparation.ca/learning-style/

Test Anxiety Secrets!

https://www.test-preparation.ca/test-anxiety/

Time Management on a Test

https://www.test-preparation.ca/time-management/

Flash Cards - The Complete Guide

https://www.test-preparation.ca/flash-cards/

How to Memorize - The Complete Guide

https://www.test-preparation.ca/memorize/

www.ingramcontent.com/pod-product-compliance
Lightning Source LLC
Chambersburg PA
CBHW071811080526
44589CB00012B/748